# SOURCES, STORIES, AND SONGS

## READ ALOUD ANTHOLOGY

# Communities

## ADVENTURES IN TIME AND PLACE

SOURCES, STORIES, AND SONGS

READ ALOUD ANTHOLOGY

# Communities

## ADVENTURES IN TIME AND PLACE

- Biographies and Autobiographies
- Folk Tales and Fables
- Interviews
- Journals and Diaries
- Letters
- Nonfiction Selections
- Plays
- Poems
- Songs
- Stories
- Visual Documents

McGraw-Hill
School Division

New York          Farmington

## PROGRAM AUTHORS

**Dr. James A. Banks**
Professor of Education and Director of the Center for Multicultural Education
University of Washington
Seattle, Washington

**Dr. Barry K. Beyer**
Professor Emeritus, Graduate School of Education
George Mason University
Fairfax, Virginia

**Dr. Gloria Contreras**
Professor of Education
University of North Texas
Denton, Texas

**Jean Craven**
District Coordinator of Curriculum Development
Albuquerque Public Schools
Albuquerque, New Mexico

**Dr. Gloria Ladson-Billings**
Professor of Education
University of Wisconsin
Madison, Wisconsin

**Dr. Mary A. McFarland**
Instructional Coordinator of Social Studies, K–12, and Director of Staff Development
Parkway School District
Chesterfield, Missouri

**Dr. Walter C. Parker**
Professor and Program Chair for Social Studies Education
University of Washington
Seattle, Washington

**NATIONAL GEOGRAPHIC SOCIETY**
Washington, D.C.

## Acknowledgments

"Why We Have Dogs in Hopi Villages" from AND IT IS STILL THAT WAY Legends told by Arizona Indian Children with notes by Byrd Baylor. ©1976 by Byrd Baylor. Published by Trails West Press, Santa Fe, New Mexico.

Excerpts from WHAT ARE YOU FIGURING NOW? A STORY ABOUT BENJAMIN BANNEKER by Jeri Ferris. Text ©1988 by Jeri Ferris. Published by Carolrhoda Books, Inc., Minneapolis, MN.

"En un barrio de Los Angeles"/"In a Neighborhood in Los Angeles" from CUERPO EN LLAMAS/BODY IN FLAMES by Francisco X. Alarcón. Chronicle Books.

"In Good Old Colony Times" from THE FOLKSONGS OF NORTH AMERICA. © 1960 by Alan Lomax. Published by Doubleday & Company, Inc., Garden City, New York.

"Picking Berries" from OUT IN THE DARK AND DAYLIGHT by Aileen Fisher. ©1980 by Aileen Fisher. HarperCollins Publishers.

Excerpts from CHILDTIMES A Three-Generation Memoir by Elise Greenfield and Lessie Jones Little. ©1956 by Ellise Greenfield and Lessie Jones Little. HarperCollins Publishers.

"Assembly-line Worker" from ALL IN A DAY'S WORK by Neil Johnson. ©1989 by Neil Johnson. Little, Brown and Company.

Text of Chapter 7 "Julio in the Lion's Den" from CLASS PRESIDENT by Johanna Hurwitz. Text ©1990 by Johanna Hurwitz. Morrow Junior Books, a division of William Morrow & Company, Inc.

(continued on page 141)

## McGraw-Hill School Division
*A Division of The McGraw-Hill Companies*

McGraw-Hill School Division
1221 Avenue of the Americas
New York, New York 10020

Printed in the United States of America

ISBN 0-02-147582-2 / 3

3 4 5 6 7 8 9 079 03 02 01 00

# TABLE OF *Contents*

# USING PRIMARY SOURCES AND LITERATURE WITH SOCIAL STUDIES

The readings in the *Adventures in Time and Place Anthology* have been carefully selected to enhance social studies concepts and to provide enjoyable and worthwhile reading experiences for students. All readers bring to the reading experience their own backgrounds and prior knowledge. Exposing students to a variety of viewpoints while encouraging them to question and ponder what they read will help them to become critical readers and thoughtful citizens.

The readings include **primary sources, secondary sources,** and **literature.** These fall into several categories, including:

- songs
- stories
- oral histories
- plays
- interviews
- poems
- folk tales
- nonfiction stories
- autobiographies and biographies
- photographs and graphics

The readings offer you a unique teaching tool. The following suggestions will help your students use the readings to build and extend their knowledge of social studies as well as to sharpen their analytical skills.

## PRIMARY AND SECONDARY SOURCES

A **primary source** is something that comes from the time that is being studied. Primary sources include such things as official documents of the time, diaries and journals, letters, newspaper articles and advertisements, photographs, and oral histories. A **secondary source** is an account of the past written by someone who was not an eyewitness to those events. Remind students of the difference between primary and secondary sources. Point out that primary sources give historians valuable clues from the past because they provide firsthand information about a certain time or event. Primary sources let the reader see how people lived, felt, and thought.

However, primary sources express the view of only one person. Thus, it is important for students to understand the point of view of the writer and to find out all that they can about his or her background to decide whether the writer is credible, or believable. Secondary sources often compare and analyze different points of view and give a broader view of the event. Once again, however, it is important for students to understand the writer's point of view and analyze his or her credentials.

Suggest to students that, when they read primary and secondary sources, they ask themselves these questions:

- Who created the source?
- Can the writer be believed?
- Does the writer have expert knowledge of the subject?
- Does the writer have a reason to describe the events in a certain way?
- Does the writer have a reputation for being accurate?

When you work with the primary sources in this Anthology, you may wish to encourage students to think about the following as they read some of the various sources:

**Autobiographies** What role did the subject of the autobiography play in history? How was the person influenced by the time in which he or she lived?

**Diaries and Journals** Was the diary or journal originally written to be shared with the public? What is the writer's point of view?

**Interviews** Who is the person being interviewed? What is his or her point of view?

**Letters** What is the purpose of the letter? To whom was it written?

## LITERATURE

In social studies, literature is used to motivate and instruct. It also plays a large role in assisting students to understand their cultural heritage and the cultural heritage of others. For example, the songs, stories, and poetry of different cultures offer students opportunities to compare and contrast and, hence, understand aspects of cultural identity. Plays, especially those written to reflect social studies concepts and historical information, afford students opportunities to work together cooperatively on a production while learning valuable content. Nonfiction selections, such as ... *If You Were There When They Signed the Constitution*, give students an opportunity to step back into an historical period and view that time from the point of view of someone "who was there."

Suggest to students that, as they read the literature selections, they ask themselves these questions:

- *Who* is the author of the selection?
- *What* is the author's background?
- *What* is the author's purpose and point of view?

In *Communities* you will be reading about many different people, places, and times. This Anthology, or collection of writings by different people, will make the information in your textbook come to life in a special way. The Anthology includes stories, tall tales, songs, biographies, poems, posters, interviews, letters, diaries, and plays. As you read these selections, you will be able to see, feel, and hear what it is like to live in other communities. Your Anthology will even take you back into the past and help you feel what it was like to live in other times! The selections in your Anthology will help you to better understand communities in the past and present, both near and far.

**INTRODUCTION •**
Gives you background information about the selection and tells you what kind of writing it is. Is it fiction or nonfiction? Is it a poem or a song? The introduction also asks you a question to think about as you read the selection.

**DEFINITIONS •**
Gives you the meanings of difficult words

**CONCLUSION •**
Provides additional information and asks you to think further about the selection

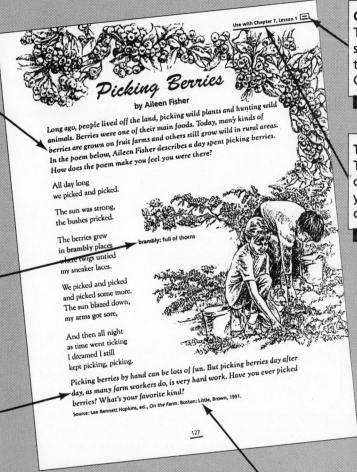

**CASSETTE LOGO •**
Tells you that the selection appears on the Anthology Cassette

**TEXTBOOK LINK •**
Tells you which chapter and lesson in your textbook the document is linked to

**SOURCE •**
Tells you where the selection came from

# LIVING TOGETHER IN COMMUNITIES

*On summer evenings the boys liked to sit on their porch watching the river and making up stories about it. Where, they wondered, did the river begin.*

from *Where the River Begins*
by Thomas Locker

# The Town That Moved

## by Mary Jane Finsand

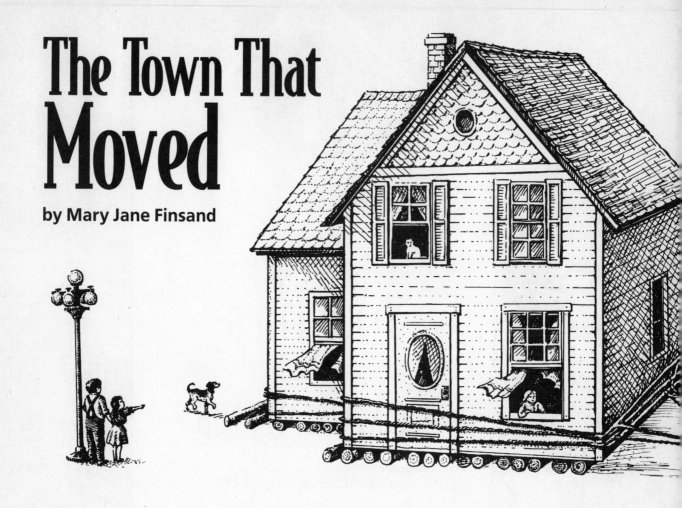

*When people in a community work together, the most difficult problems can be solved. More than a hundred years ago, the town of Hibbing, Minnesota, proved this to be true. Hibbing was built in 1893 after iron ore was discovered in the area. Iron ore is an important natural resource. In the 1800s iron was especially needed for building railroad tracks and trains. This selection from a true story begins after the discovery of iron ore in Minnesota. As people move to the area to work in the iron ore mines, a community begins to grow. What is the main problem the townspeople must solve? How are they able to solve it?*

It wasn't long before news of the **iron ore** in Minnesota had spread all around the country. Men began to pour into Minnesota. They came to start iron ore **mines**.

One of those men was named Frank Hibbing. Frank Hibbing knew that if he started an iron ore mine he would need many men to work in it. The men would want to bring their families. So Hibbing decided to build a town.

**iron ore:** rock from which we get **iron**

**iron:** important metal used in making steel

**mines:** large areas dug under the ground for digging out minerals

2

First he bought land. Then he hired men to build roads. He hired other men to build log cabins for the families.

Soon people were coming from all over the country to work in Hibbing's mine and live in his town.

People even came from countries far away like Ireland, Sweden, and Germany. Many came to work in the mine, but others came to open stores. Soon there were schools and churches and banks too. On August 15, 1893, the people voted to become the town of Hibbing, Minnesota.

Hibbing became famous for its rich iron ore. The town grew and grew. Everyone who lived there was very proud of Hibbing. They wanted to make it a beautiful city. They built fancy theaters and lovely parks and fine houses. They started excellent schools for their children, and they took wonderful care of their town.

Then one day the mine owners made a discovery: THE VERY BEST IRON ORE WAS RIGHT BENEATH THE TOWN OF HIBBING! The people of Hibbing would have to move. If they didn't, the mines would have to shut down. The miners would be out of work. Soon the other businesses would have to close down too.

The people of Hibbing were very upset. They had worked so hard to build their beautiful town. How could they leave it? How could they watch it be torn down to make way for new mines? "Where will we go?" they asked.

"We will build you a new town," said the mine owners.

"But what about our fine homes and our fancy theaters and our beautiful hotels?" the people asked.

The mine owners thought and thought, and finally they came up with a solution. "We will move your homes!" they said. "We will move the whole town!" It sounded like a wonderful idea. But how on earth would they do it?

The mine owners and the people sat down together to think and talk.

"We have horses and tractors," said one man. "Maybe we could pull the buildings."

"But we can't pull big buildings along the ground," said the mayor. "They will break into pieces. We need wheels or something."

"Wheels are a problem," said the mine owners. "Most of our wheels are just not large or strong enough to move a building."

"Well," said someone else, "we certainly have lots of trees. We could cut them down, and then make them smooth and roll our houses on them."

"That's it!" everyone cried.

So the mine owners and the people began to get ready for moving day. They separated all the buildings from their basements.

Then they dug new basements for all those buildings. They chopped down trees. Then they cut away the branches. They made the logs smooth.

People all over the world heard about Hibbing's plan to move. "Impossible!" they said. One big city newspaper wrote: "HIBBING GONE CRAZY!" No one believed that the people of Hibbing could move their whole town.

Finally moving day arrived. The Hibbing Hotel would be the first building moved. The miners attached large chains and ropes to cranes from the mine. The cranes would be powered by steam engines. Then the chains were wrapped over and under the Hibbing Hotel. Slowly the cranes lifted the hotel. Then they swung it over and lowered it gently onto a log roller.

Next ropes and straps were wrapped around the hotel, then attached to horses up front. "Giddap! Giddap!" shouted the horse drivers. The horses started forward. Slowly the Hibbing Hotel rolled down the street.

As soon as the back log rolled out from under the building, people grabbed it. They strapped it to a horse and pulled it up to the front. Then they slid it underneath again.

After the Hibbing Hotel was moved, they moved the Oliver Clubhouse. The Oliver was so big, it had to be cut in two parts to move it.

Down the street the buildings rolled to their new locations. Day in and day out the people of Hibbing worked to save their beautiful town. At last all the business buildings had been moved. Next would come the houses.

"What should we do with our furniture?" the women asked.

"And our toys and clothes," said the children.

"Leave everything in the houses," they were told. "And you can ride in your houses too."

The very next day the first house was lifted onto logs. Down the street it came. A log was placed up front. Then a log rolled out back. That log was placed up front, and another log rolled out back. And so it went until, one after another, 186 houses had been moved.

The people of Hibbing had done it! They had moved their whole town!

*Communities must grow and change in order to survive. What changes have you noticed in your own community?*

Source: Mary Jane Finsand, *The Town That Moved*. Minneapolis: Carolrhoda Books, 1983.

# All the Places to Love

## by Patricia MacLachlan

*All the Places to Love by Patricia MacLachlan tells the story of a boy living in a rural community. Notice the many details and images the writer uses to show the relationship between nature and the boy's family. What do the different family members love most about their rural community?*

On the day I was born
My grandmother wrapped me in a blanket
   made from the wool of her sheep.
She held me up in the open window
So that what I heard first was the wind.
What I saw first were all the places to love:
The valley,
The river falling down over rocks,
The hilltop where the blueberries grew.
My grandfather was painting the barn,
And when he saw me he cried.

He carved my name—ELI—
On a **rafter** beside his name
And Grandmother's name
And the names of my papa and mama.
Mama carried me on her shoulders before I could walk,
Through the meadows and hay fields.
The cows watched us and the sheep scattered;
The dogs ran ahead, looking back with sly smiles.
When the grass was high
Only their tails showed.
When I was older, Papa and I plowed the fields.
*Where else is soil so sweet?* he said.
Once Papa and I lay down in the field, holding hands,
And the birds surrounded us:
**Raucous** black **grackles**, redwings,
Crows in the dirt that **swaggered** like pirates.
When we left, Papa put a handful of dirt in his pocket.
I did too.
My grandmother loved the river best
    of all the places to love.
*That sound, like a whisper*, she said;
Gathering in pools
Where trout flashed like jewels in the sunlight.
Grandmother sailed little bark boats downriver to me
With messages.
*I Love You Eli*, one said.
We jumped from rock to rock to rock,
Across the river to where the woods began,
Where **bunchberry** grew under the pine-needle path
And **trillium** bloomed.
Under the beech tree was a soft, rounded bed
    where a deer had slept.
The bed was warm when I touched it.
When spring rains came and the meadow turned to
    **marsh,**

**rafter:** one of the beams that support a roof

**raucous:** noisy
**grackles:** blackbirds
**swaggered:** walked boldly

**bunchberry:** woody, flowering herb
**trillium:** flower with three petals

**marsh:** wet land

**Cattails** stood like guards, and **killdeers** called.

Ducks nested by **marsh marigolds,**

And the old turtle—his shell all worn—

No matter how slow,

Still surprised me.

Sometimes we climbed to the place Mama loved best,

With our blueberry buckets and a chair for my
    grandmother:

To the blueberry **barren** where no trees grew—

The sky an arm's length away;

Where marsh hawks **skimmed** over the land,

And bears came to eat fruit,

And wild turkeys left footprints for us to find,

Like messages.

*Where else,* said my mama, *can I see the sun rise on one side*

*And the sun set on the other?*

My grandfather's barn is sweet-smelling
    and dark and cool;

Leather **harnesses** hang like paintings against old wood

And hay dust floats like gold in the air.

Grandfather once lived in the city,

And once he lived by the sea;

But the barn is the place he loves most.

*Where else,* he says, *can the soft sound of cows chewing*

*Make all the difference in the world?*

Today we wait, him sitting on a wooden-slat chair

And me on the hay,

Until, much later, my grandmother holds up a small
    bundle in the open window,

Wrapped in a blanket made from the wool of her sheep,

And my grandfather cries.

Together

We carve the name *SYLVIE* in the rafter

Beside the names of Grandfather and Grandmother,

And my mama and papa,

**cattails:** tall marsh
    plants

**killdeers:** wading birds

**marsh marigolds:** plants
    that grow in damp
    areas

**barren:** land with few
    plants

**skimmed:** flew lightly

**harnesses:** straps used
    to attach animals to
    the loads they pull

And me.

My sister is born.

Someday I might live in the city.
Someday I might live by the sea.
But soon I will carry Sylvie on my
    shoulders through the fields;
I will send her messages downriver in small boats;
And I will watch her at the top of the hill,
Trying to touch the sky.
I will show her my favorite place, the marsh,
Where ducklings follow their mother
Like tiny **tumbles** of leaves.

**tumbles:** groups

All the places to love are here, I'll tell her,
    no matter where you may live.
*Where else,* I will say, *does an old turtle crossing the path*
*Make all the difference in the world?*

**Why do you think that Eli wants to tell his sister that a turtle crossing the path makes "all the difference in the world"? Why do you think he finds such a small thing so important?**

Source: Patricia MacLachlan, *All the Places to Love*. New York: HarperCollins, 1994.

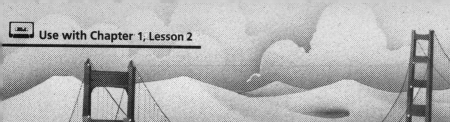

# City Poems
## by Langston Hughes

*Sometimes we get so used to the special features in our community that we hardly notice them anymore. We expect to see the mountains or skyscrapers or houses—or whatever it is that we are used to—and so we do not give them very much thought. Then perhaps when we take a trip to a different community, we do notice its features. The poet Langston Hughes took a trip to San Francisco, California, and wrote about what he saw. San Francisco is surrounded by the beautiful waters of San Francisco Bay and the Pacific Ocean. What features of the city does Langston Hughes write about in these two poems?*

## City: San Francisco

In the morning the city
Spreads its wings
Making a song
In stone that sings.

In the evening the city
Goes to bed
Hanging lights
About its head.

## Trip: San Francisco

I went to San Francisco.
I saw the bridges high
Spun across the water
Like cobwebs in the sky.

*There are two good reasons to write about your community. One is that it can help you to describe it to other people. Another is that it can help you to see the details for yourself. How does Hughes help us to see what he saw? Suppose you were seeing your own community for the first time. What do you think you would notice?*

Source: *America Forever Now.* New York: Crowell, 1968.

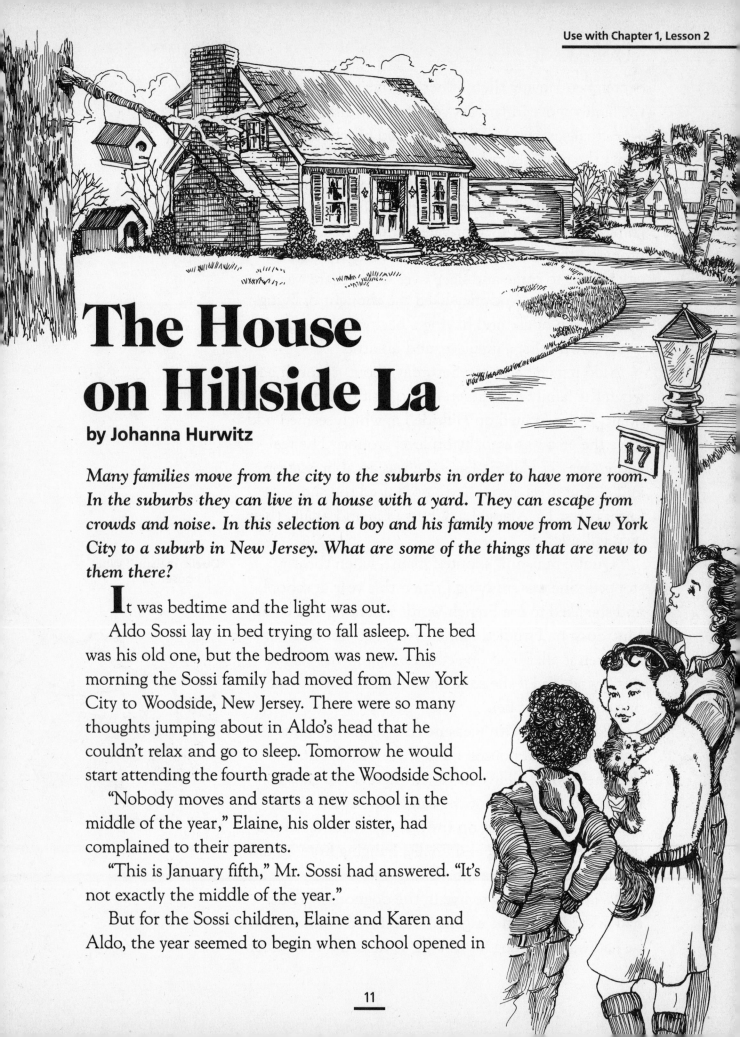

# The House on Hillside La

**by Johanna Hurwitz**

*Many families move from the city to the suburbs in order to have more room. In the suburbs they can live in a house with a yard. They can escape from crowds and noise. In this selection a boy and his family move from New York City to a suburb in New Jersey. What are some of the things that are new to them there?*

It was bedtime and the light was out.

Aldo Sossi lay in bed trying to fall asleep. The bed was his old one, but the bedroom was new. This morning the Sossi family had moved from New York City to Woodside, New Jersey. There were so many thoughts jumping about in Aldo's head that he couldn't relax and go to sleep. Tomorrow he would start attending the fourth grade at the Woodside School.

"Nobody moves and starts a new school in the middle of the year," Elaine, his older sister, had complained to their parents.

"This is January fifth," Mr. Sossi had answered. "It's not exactly the middle of the year."

But for the Sossi children, Elaine and Karen and Aldo, the year seemed to begin when school opened in

September. Having their father change jobs and make the family move in January seemed very difficult.

Actually, when Mr. Sossi had told his children about the proposed move to New Jersey, it had seemed very exciting. Elaine and Karen, who were fourteen and twelve and a half, were delighted that they were going to have their own private rooms. Their mother promised the children that they could invite their old city friends to come and sleep over when there was a school vacation. And they liked the thought of living in their own house and having a backyard, an upstairs and a downstairs, a fireplace, and an attic.

Aldo remembered the Saturday about a month ago when the family had driven out to visit their new home. It was located on Hillside La, which seemed odd since the area was actually on level ground. The real address was 17 Hillside Lane. *La* was an abbreviation, and all the street signs they passed used the short form: Forest La, Maple La, Cherry La, and finally their own Hillside La.

**"Quelle maison!"** shouted Elaine, when the car stopped. She was studying French this year at school, and she liked to use French words whenever she could. Mrs. Sossi had studied French years ago but had forgotten it all. So no one could be sure what Elaine was saying, and if she sometimes made a mistake, no one could correct her.

**Quelle maison!: What a house!**

Aldo noticed with pleasure that their new house was really several houses. First, there was the house that they would all live in. Then there was a garage, which was the house for the car. In the city they had just parked the car out on the street. There was also a doghouse in the yard, and finally, hanging from an old maple tree, there was a little birdhouse.

"Will we get a dog to live in the doghouse?" Aldo had asked his parents eagerly. Aldo loved animals, and he had wanted a dog for as long as he could remember.

"I don't know. Let's wait and see how things work out," said his mother. "Maybe the cats will want the house for themselves," she said. The Sossi family had two cats, Peabody and Poughkeepsie.

"Will the cats go outdoors?" wondered Karen. In the city the cats were always kept inside the apartment. Life in the suburbs was obviously going to mean a lot of changes for them all, even the cats.

They had gone inside, and each of the Sossi children had picked out a bedroom. It was fun walking through the empty rooms and hearing their voices echoing as they called out their discoveries to one another.

"**Voila!**" Elaine shouted. "This room has a window seat!"

**Voila!:** There it is!

Karen found a closet that was so big it had a window inside it.

Aldo was interested in everything. He went down to the basement, where there was a furnace and a washing machine and a dryer. He **investigated** the attic, which had nothing in it but dust and old spider webs.

**investigated:** searched carefully

Mrs. Sossi was **mentally** moving all their furniture about. "Let's put the sofa here." She pointed to one area of the living room. "And we can put the television over here."

**mentally:** in the mind

It had been a very exciting day, and Aldo, watching squirrels chase one another up and down the maple tree in the backyard, had tried not to think how nervous he would feel when the time came to start the new school.

*Aldo worries about starting a new school and making new friends. Do you think moving is difficult for this reason? What other changes might be hard to get used to? Suppose your family could move to a different kind of community. Would you want to move? Why or why not?*

Source: Johanna Hurwitz, *Aldo Applesauce*. New York: William Morrow, 1979.

# The City Blues

## American Folk Blues

*Have you ever heard people say they had the blues? They meant they were feeling sad or lonely. The blues is also a kind of music first sung by African Americans. Many blues songs tell about sad and hard times. Other blues songs are not sad at all. Here is a blues song about visiting unfamiliar cities for the first time. How do you think the traveler feels?*

1. Cloud - y in the west, Looks like rain;___ I spent all my mon - ey on the sub - way train__ in New York Ci - ty,___ In New York Ci - ty,___ In New York Ci - ty, you real - ly got to know your way.___

2. Went to Detroit, it was fine,
   I watched the cars movin' off
     th' assembly line,
   In Detroit City, In Detroit City,
   In Detroit City, you really got
     to know your way.

3. I looped the loop, I rocked and reeled,
   I thought the Cubs played ball
     in Marshall Field,
   In the Windy City, in the Windy City,
   In the Windy City, you really got
     to know your way.

4. Went a little south, St. Louis (Loo-ee),
   A piece of Missouri on the Mississippi,
   In old St. Louis, in old St. Louis,
   In old St. Louis, you really got
     to know your way.

5. I moved on down, New Orleans (Or-leens).
   I had my first taste of its pecan pralines,
   In New Orleans, in New Orleans,
   In New Orleans, you really got
     to know your way.

6. I headed West, to "L.A."
   It really is a city where it's fun to stay,
   In old "L.A.," in old "L.A.,"
   In old "L.A.." you really got
     to know your way.

7. Headed up the coast, "Golden Gate."
   I went out to the wharf to eat a
     "Fisherman's Plate,"
   In San Francisco, in San Francisco,
   In San Francisco, you really got
     to know your way.

14

# Where the River Begins

## by Thomas Locker

*When water flows from one place to another, a river is formed. Rivers flow into larger rivers or into other bodies of water, such as lakes and oceans. But where do rivers begin? In this story, two boys try to find out where the river that runs past their house begins. Join them on this exciting journey into the mountains. As you read, notice the different ways the author describes the river. How does the river change as the boys get closer to where it begins?*

**O**nce there were two boys named Josh and Aaron who lived with their family in a big yellow house. Nearby was a river that flowed gently into the sea. On summer evenings the boys liked to sit on their porch watching the river and making up stories about it. Where, they wondered, did the river begin.

Their grandfather loved the river and had lived near it all his life. Perhaps he would know. One day

Josh and Aaron asked their grandfather to take them on a camping trip to find the beginning of the river. When he agreed, they made plans and began to pack. They started out early the next morning. For a time they walked along a familiar road past fields of golden wheat and sheep grazing in the sun. Nearby flowed the river—gentle, wide, and deep.

At last they reached the **foothills** of the mountains. The road had ended and now the river would be their only guide. It raced over rocks and **boulders** and had become so narrow that the boys and their grandfather could jump across.

**foothills:** low hills at the bottom of a mountain

**boulders:** large rocks

In the late afternoon, while the sun was still hot, the river led them into a dark forest. They found a **campsite** and set up their tent. Then the boys went wading in the cold river water.

**campsite:** place to camp

The first long day away from home was over. That night, around the flickering campfire, their grandfather told Josh and Aaron stories. Drifting off to sleep, they listened to the forest noises and were **soothed** by the sound of the river.

**soothed:** calmed

**Dawn** seemed to come quickly and the sun glowed through a thick mist. The boys were eager to be off, but their grandfather was stiff from sleeping on the ground and was slower getting started.

**dawn:** the beginning of day

The path they chose led them high above the river. On a grassy **knoll** they stopped to gaze around. The morning mist had risen and formed white clouds in the sky. In the distance the river **meandered** lazily. It was so narrow that it seemed almost to disappear. They all felt a great excitement, for they knew they were nearing the end of their journey.

**knoll:** small, round hill

**meandered:** followed a winding course

Without a word the boys began to run. They followed the river for an hour or more until it **trickled** into a still pond, high in an **upland** meadow. In this small, peaceful place the river began. Finally their search was over. As they started back, the sky suddenly darkened.

**trickled:** flowed slowly

**upland:** high land

Thunder crashed around them and lightning lit the sky. They **pitched** their tent and crawled inside just before the storm broke. Rain pounded on the roof of their small tent all night long, but they were warm and dry inside.

**pitched:** set up

In the morning long before dawn they were awakened by a roaring, rushing sound. The river had **swelled** with the storm and was flooding its **banks**. They tried to take a shortcut across a field but were soon ankle deep in water. Grandfather explained that the river drew its waters from the rains high up in the mountains.

**swelled:** risen higher
**banks:** edges

They came down out of the foothills in the soft light of late afternoon. The boys recognized the cliffs along the river and knew they were close to home. Their **weariness** lifted and they began to move more quickly down the road.

**weariness:** tired feeling

At last they reached their house on the hill. The boys raced ahead to tell their mother and father about the place where the river began. But their grandfather paused for a moment and in the fading light he watched the river, which continued on as it always had, flowing gently into the sea.

*As you read this story, could you picture the river when it was gentle and wide? Could you imagine it when it was fast and narrow? How could the same river be lazy and winding at one point and roaring and rushing at another? What else in nature changes shape or speed?*

Source: Thomas Locker, *Where the River Begins.* New York: Dial, 1984.

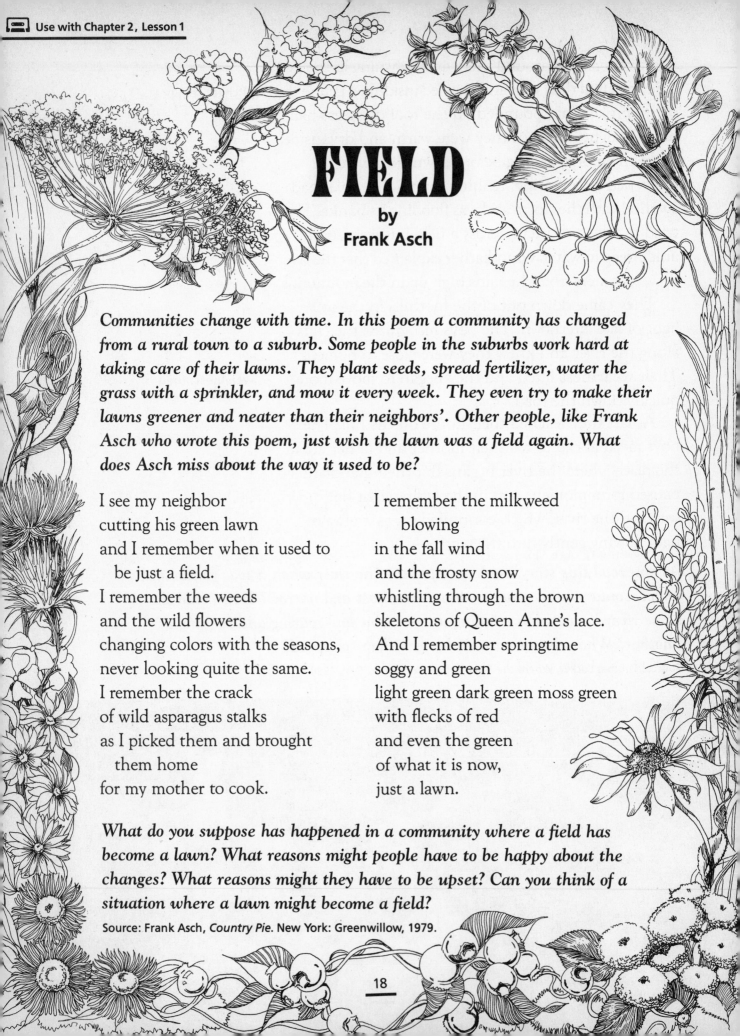

# FIELD

## by
## Frank Asch

*Communities change with time. In this poem a community has changed from a rural town to a suburb. Some people in the suburbs work hard at taking care of their lawns. They plant seeds, spread fertilizer, water the grass with a sprinkler, and mow it every week. They even try to make their lawns greener and neater than their neighbors'. Other people, like Frank Asch who wrote this poem, just wish the lawn was a field again. What does Asch miss about the way it used to be?*

I see my neighbor
cutting his green lawn
and I remember when it used to
  be just a field.
I remember the weeds
and the wild flowers
changing colors with the seasons,
never looking quite the same.
I remember the crack
of wild asparagus stalks
as I picked them and brought
  them home
for my mother to cook.

I remember the milkweed
  blowing
in the fall wind
and the frosty snow
whistling through the brown
skeletons of Queen Anne's lace.
And I remember springtime
soggy and green
light green dark green moss green
with flecks of red
and even the green
of what it is now,
just a lawn.

*What do you suppose has happened in a community where a field has become a lawn? What reasons might people have to be happy about the changes? What reasons might they have to be upset? Can you think of a situation where a lawn might become a field?*

Source: Frank Asch, *Country Pie*. New York: Greenwillow, 1979.

# Dear World

## Edited by Lannis Temple

*One day a Texan named Lannis Temple had an exciting idea. He decided to travel around the world and ask children to discuss their thoughts about nature and the environment. As you read a few of the children's letters from Temple's book, think about what you would like to tell people about our environment.*

Dear People of the Whole World:
My best experience in the outdoors was when I went to the sea. I think it's really fun at the beach because you can collect shells and you can also find all kinds of animals there. I feel really nice inside then. I really like it too when the wind blows in my face, and when the sand tickles me between my toes.

*Jacky Jacobs*, Age 11
The Netherlands

Dear World,
My favorite part of nature is the mountains. I love to sit on top of the mountains and look down, and see our world below me. I love the amazing views that you witness while on the mountain. Being there makes me feel a part of nature most of all. The crisp, cold breeze chills your body but never chills your soul which contains the everlasting love of nature.
I also have many fears about nature's future. If man kills the green, there won't be enough oxygen....
I dream that people will notice that in order for their children to live a good life, they must treat the world like their own children.

With love and peace
Jonathan Lee, Age 10
Dallas, Texas, USA

I love in nature the sky, the trees, sunset flowers blooming, colourful butterflies and birds that sing in the morning.
I love to sit under tall trees.
I love to look at the sky during the night.
I love to climb up the mountains and ski down the snow.
I love animals big and small.
I love to eat my food while sitting on the green grass.
I love to play in the fresh air.
I feel that I am a big part of nature and I will keep taking care of it.
I do not like the water becoming polluted with dirt and bad things.
I don't like the air to be polluted with petrol.
I also hope that nature will remain beautiful and clean and that animals will not die from flooding.
I also hope that the earth will not melt.

With compliments, your true friend
*Shadieh Khalaf Al-Tawil*, Age 11
West Bank

To everyone in the world!
I would like to set up a day when no one drives their cars.

*Chiecko Nakayomo*, Age 11
Hiroshima, Japan

*Shadieh Khalaf Al-Tawil wrote, "I feel that I am a big part of nature and I will keep taking care of it." In what way are people "a part of nature"? What are some things you can do to help take care of nature?*

Source: Lannis Temple, ed., *Dear World: How Children Around the World Feel About Our Environment*. New York: Random House, 1993.

# 50
# Simple Things Kids Can Do To Recycle

## by the EarthWorks Group

*You probably know that recycling saves energy as well as natural resources. But according to this sequel to the book* 50 Simple Things Kids Can Do to Save the Earth, *we are still only recycling between 10 and 15 percent of our garbage. Every three months, the book tells us, Americans throw out enough aluminum to rebuild every plane in our airlines. What are some other things that can be made from recycled materials?*

### A CLEAR CHOICE
### Take a Guess.

*How many times can you recycle a glass bottle?*

**A)** *Once*    **B)** *25 times*    **C)** *An unlimited number of times*

**Y**ou may not realize it, but there's something in your refrigerator that's so old, George Washington or Abraham Lincoln could have used it.

Is it last week's leftovers? That weird, moldy green stuff in a bowl? Nope. It's the *glass* in the bottles and jars.

Believe it or not, people have been using—and *recycling*—glass for almost 3,000 years! Now you can be part of that history by recycling *your* empty bottles and jars, too.

**Answer: C.** Glass can be recycled over and over and over and over . . .

## RECYCLING FACTS

- Glass is usually made by mixing sand with a few other natural ingredients (soda, feldspar and limestone). The mixture is put into a very hot furnace and when it melts, it turns to glass. Heating the furnace takes a lot of energy.
- Glass can *also* be made by melting down *old* glass (such as bottles and jars). This is better for the Earth, because recycled glass melts at a lower temperature than new material—so it takes less energy to heat the furnace.
- For example: Recycling just one bottle can save enough energy to light a 100-watt light bulb for 4 hours!
- Making glass from recycled jars and bottles creates less air pollution, too . . . and it uses fewer natural resources. For every ton (that's 2,000 pounds) of glass that gets recycled, we save a ton of the raw materials it would take to make new glass.

## HOW TO RECYCLE GLASS

- When you finish with a bottle or jar, lightly rinse it out with water. (You don't have to wash it with soap.) Leftover food or drinks attract ants and other pests.
- Don't forget to take off caps or lids. They can't be recycled with the glass. (If they're metal, recycle them with aluminum or steel. If they're plastic, throw them out.)
- It's okay to leave on paper and plastic labels—they burn or blow off when the glass is recycled.
- "Neck rings"—the part of the bottle caps that are still on the bottlenecks—can be left on, too.
- Wash off sand and dirt from bottles you find in parks, beaches, etc. Even one little stone can ruin a whole load of recycled glass!

## IT'S OLD NEWS
### Take a Guess.
*What can be made from recycled newspapers?*
**A)** *Cereal boxes*  **B)** *Construction paper*  **C)** *More newspapers*

**S**top the presses!

Here's some important recycling news: "Experts have discovered that newspapers take up more space in our landfills than any other item!"

You can help fight this garbage problem—and save millions of trees at the same time.

How? By recycling newspapers instead of throwing them away.

## RECYCLING FACTS

- Experts say that Americans buy an average of 62 million newspapers every day—and throw away 44 million of them! That means we throw out as many as 500,000 trees' worth of newspapers *every week*.
- But we can save trees instead, because the paper used in these newspapers—called "newsprint"—can be recycled.
- Factories recycle newspapers by adding water and chemicals to them, then stirring the mixture into a kind of "soup."
- Next, they put the "soup" into paper-making machines that spray it across big screens and dry it with hot air. When it comes out, it's ready to be used in newspapers again.
- Recycling newspapers cuts air pollution and saves energy. For example: It takes half as much energy to recycle newsprint as it takes to make newsprint fresh from trees.

**Answer: A, B, C.** Newspapers can also become egg cartons, insulation, and lots more!

## HOW TO RECYCLE
- Almost any recycling center will take newspapers.
- Some want newspapers tied into bundles with string. Others want them stacked in boxes or paper bags. Call your local center to see what they prefer.
- If you have to tie newspapers, here's an easy way to do it:
  - ✓ Lay two pieces of string on the floor in a cross.
  - ✓ Put a small stack of papers (about a foot high) on top, pull the strings up, and tie them in a knot.

## RECYCLING TIPS
- Anything that comes with the newspaper (shiny colored pages, store ads, etc.) can be recycled. But don't add anything extra. "Junk mail" or magazines must be recycled separately.
- If you've used newspaper for art projects or to line your pet hamster's cage, don't recycle it—throw it out.
- Want to find out more about newspaper recycling? Write to:

    *The Newspaper Association of America*
    11600 Sunrise Valley Drive
    Reston, VA 22091
    Attn: Communications Dept.

***Look around your neighborhood. What could you and your friends do to start or improve a recycling project?***

Source: John Javna, *50 Simple Things Kids Can Do to Recycle*. Berkeley: EarthWorks Press, 1990.

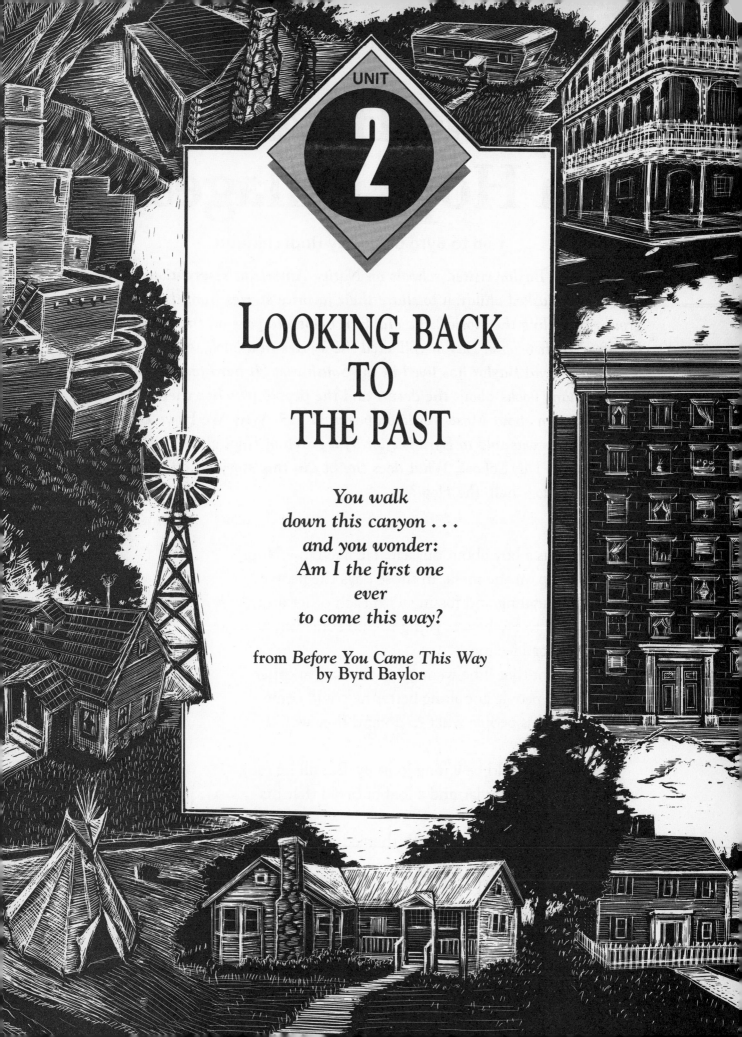

# LOOKING BACK TO THE PAST

*You walk
down this canyon . . .
and you wonder:
Am I the first one
ever
to come this way?*

from *Before You Came This Way*
by Byrd Baylor

# Why We Have Dogs in Hopi Villages

### told to Byrd Baylor by Hopi children

*Author Byrd Baylor visited schools on Native American reservations in Arizona and asked children to share their favorite stories from their Indian group. By telling the stories, the children helped to pass on the customs and beliefs of their people. Baylor collected the stories in a book, And It Is Still That Way. Byrd Baylor has lived in the Southwest all her life. She has written many books about the desert and the people who live there. You can read her poem about Mesa Verde on pages 32–35. Why We Have Dogs in Hopi Villages was told to Byrd Baylor by a group of Hopi children from the Second Mesa Day School. What does the boy in this story set off to learn? How do the dogs help the Hopi?*

There was a boy about our age. He lived in a Hopi village way up on the mesa. In those days the people were always arguing and fussing with each other and this boy used to say he was going to find some way to stop all that bad feeling.

He thought that if he went away and saw another village where people got along better he could come back and tell his people what to do and they would thank him.

He knew it would be a long journey. But all he took with him was a water jar and a loaf of bread that his mother baked for him.

When he went down the path that led away from his village he did not know which way to go. He just walked where he felt like going. Day after day he walked.

After many days had passed the boy came to the edge of a village he had never seen. It seemed like a

happy place where people got along. But as he came closer he could see that it was a village of dogs, not people.

He asked the dogs if he could speak to their chief. Even though they had never seen a human before, they could tell that this boy came in peace so they let him enter their village.

They took him down the ladder into the kiva where **councils** and ceremonies are held. The dog chief sat with all his dog councilmen in a circle. The boy joined them in the circle. . . .

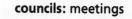councils: meetings

Then it was time to speak. The boy said, "I came to get your help so the people of my village can find out how to stop arguing and fighting all the time. Maybe some of those dogs will go back with me."

But the chief said, "It will be up to my people. I will have no part in this."

They came out of the kiva together but none of the dogs offered to go with the boy. None of them wanted to leave his own village.

When night came the boy went to a little clearing outside the village and he lay awake for a long time trying to think of a way to get the dogs to go with him.

At last a spirit came down to him from the North Star.

"What do you want?" the spirit asked. "I have all the things that you could want."

The boy did not know what to ask for. But he remembered that many of the dogs looked thin and hungry so he said, "Some food would be good."

The spirit got the food and blessed it. When the boy awoke the food was there beside him. Some of the dogs ran up to the pile of food and began to eat it.

As soon as the boy saw that the dogs were eating the blessed food he knew he had asked the spirit for the right thing. He knew he had found a way to make the dogs follow him.

He went down into the kiva again with the dog leaders of that village. . . . Then the boy told the chief, "Some of the dogs ate my food. Those are the dogs that will be willing to go with me. They belong to me now because they took my food."

It was true.

The dogs that had eaten the blessed food gathered around the boy wherever he stood. They followed him all the way to his own village up on the mesa.

He gave one dog to each family. The people were so happy to have the dogs that they stopped quarreling.

Hopi villages have been peaceful ever since.

Now dogs have their jobs here. They guard our houses and our people and go to the fields with us and watch over the sheep. And they still remind us not to quarrel. That is their main job.

*Did you notice the way this story ended? Native American storytellers like to link the past with the present. This helps to keep the old ways alive and shows the importance of the past to life today. That is why Indian storytellers often end their stories with something like "And it is still that way."*

Source: Byrd Baylor, *And It Is Still That Way.* New York: Scribner's, 1976.

# EAGLE DRUM

## by Robert Crum

*A powwow is a traditional Native American ceremony that includes dancing, feasting, and celebration. Nine-year-old Louis Pierre is a member of the Pend Oreille (PAHND uh RAY) people of Montana. He has learned traditional Native American dances from his grandfather, Pat. Author Robert Crum spent a summer with Louis and the Pierre family, traveling with them from powwow to powwow. In this selection from Crum's book about Louis's experience on the powwow trail, Louis, his brother Michael, his uncle David, and Pat are on their way to dance in a powwow. What do the dancers think about during the ceremony?*

Louis and his family attend between fifteen and twenty powwows a year. They often just drive down the road to dance inside the community center in the town of St. Ignatius, Montana, or to the bigger powwow grounds in the town of Arlee. But sometimes they travel as far as three hundred miles to the **reservation** of another tribe. The dances they participate in are part of the northern powwow **circuit**, which includes most of the northern Great Plains. The southern circuit is centered in Oklahoma. Some of the tribes that host the powwows have different dances and customs, but there are still a lot of similarities. And even though some dancers may be far from home when visiting a different reservation, they're always treated like friends.

**reservation:** land set aside for Native Americans

**circuit:** route

While traveling to a powwow, David puts on a tape of Indian singers. "I used to listen to rock 'n' roll, like most of the kids in my high school," he says. "But recently all I've been listening to are powwow songs."

It's about the only music that Louis listens to, also. "I sing the songs to myself sometimes when I'm walking to school," he says, "or when I'm waiting for a ball to come my way at third base, you know, during a Little League game."

Louis, Michael, and David sing along with the tape as they drive through the countryside—"singing Indian," they call it. Pat hums along, tapping his hand on the steering wheel in time to the music. Most of the songs don't have any words. They're just syllables, like *hey, ya, ha, ha, hey.* . . . The syllables keep the rhythm, while the melody lifts and falls like a hawk soaring on a wind.

They drive through forests and across high dusty plains, past cattle ranches and fields of wheat. This is the country that their people used to wander through in search of buffalo. It is where their **ancestors** are buried. Big rivers wind through the valleys. High mountains rise in the distance. In the afternoon the sky darkens with black clouds, and soon it is raining—a brief summer thunderstorm. The windshield wipers seem to keep time to the songs on the tape.

**ancestors:** relatives from long ago

Before reaching the powwow, Pat usually gives the boys a little talk. "When you're out there dancing this weekend," he says, "remember that you're not just dancing to win a contest. There are more important reasons to dance. You should pick out someone not as **fortunate** as you are, and keep them in mind when you're dancing— an elder who is too old to dance or someone who's sick or someone who has lost a loved one. If you remember to do that, your dancing will be good."

**fortunate:** lucky

The boys nod. They know what Pat is talking about. The dance arbor (the ring in the middle of a powwow where all the dancing is done) is a special place. When you're dancing in the circle of the dance arbor, whatever good thoughts you have usually come back to you.

Louis has a friend who once learned that lesson in an unforgettable way. Arriving at a powwow one day, the dancer saw an old man sitting near the entrance, with a cane in his hand and his head hanging down. The dancer thought he looked like the saddest person he'd ever seen. He waved and said, "How ya doin'?"

But the old man didn't even look up. "Not so good," he mumbled. "My legs are bad, and my dancin' days are long gone."

The dancer paused and then reached out his hand. "I'm going to be dancing for you tonight, old man," he said. The man raised his eyes and weakly shook the dancer's hand.

According to Louis's friend, that was the best night of dancing he ever had. He felt the singing and the drumming inside his body as he danced, and the colors of his **feathers and fringe** shivered in the lights. The earth felt good beneath his feet. The great sky full of stars wheeled overhead. And every now and then, he saw the old man sitting in the stands, watching him **intensely**.

When the dancing was over for the night, he walked back to his pup tent and fell into an exhausted sleep. In the morning he was suddenly awakened by someone shaking the tent. He opened the flap and looked out. It was an old woman, and she was holding out a big breakfast of eggs and toast and coffee.

"I'm the wife of the man you danced for last night," she said. "He wanted you to know that he woke up this morning feeling happier than he has in years. So we made you this breakfast. Thanks!"

**feathers and fringe:**
traditional costume

**intensely:** closely

*For Louis, being part of a Native American community means living in two worlds. Think about some of the traditions and customs of people in your community. Why do you think people keep the customs of the people who lived before them?*

Source: Robert Crum, *Eagle Drum: On the powwow trail with a young grass dancer.* New York: Four Winds, 1994.

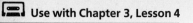 

# Before You Came This Way

## by Byrd Baylor

*Anasazi is an Indian word that means "ancient ones." The Anasazi Indians were one of the early groups who lived in the American Southwest. They built their homes out of stone, into the sides of mesas or cliffs. In this selection, author Byrd Baylor describes rock paintings that are found on the walls of these ancient homes. How do Baylor's descriptions help bring these paintings to life? How does this poem describe life in this area hundreds of years ago?*

You walk
down this canyon,
this place of
high red cliffs
and turning winds
and hawks that float
in a far white sky
and
you wonder:
"Am I the first one
ever
to come this way?"

And
you wonder
"Is my footprint

the first one
ever
to touch this sand?"

But
then you see something
which tells you,
No,
you're not the first.
Your brothers
out of some
long ago lost age
passed this way too.

You see their marks
on canyon walls.

Even the print
of their hands
is left,
chipped deep
in stone.

These men who came before you—
cliff dwellers,
hunters,
wanderers—
left messages
on rocks,
on cliff sides,
on steep rough
canyon walls.

They drew
the things
they did
and saw.
They even drew
their corn plants

and the birds
that flew above
their heads
and the paths

men cut
through nameless lands.

The reds
and yellows
and blacks
have been battered
by a thousand winds,
washed by a thousand rains.

The pictures are dim now,
half shadow,
but you search the canyon
for them.

And here
you see
young hunters
leap
in the morning sun.
The light still
gleams on their
arrows.

And here
a coyote
howls at the moon.

From his own hill
he guards his world.
He keeps the moon
in sight.

And rabbits flick
their ears
listening

listening

listening

while men do battle.
That fierce battle
raged
loud as thunder
across this canyon
Once

You find deer
with great antlers
branching like trees.

What is it they hear?

In the wind
there's the scent
of a mountain lion
who twitches his whiskers,
twitches his tail,
as he smiles
at himself. . .
or the deer.

Mountain goats
with curly horns.

Goats.
Goats.
More goats.
They drew them everywhere.
The clink of sharp hoofs
must have rung
as those goats jumped
from rock
to rock
to rock—

and then jumped back
where they had been
before. . . .

High on a rock
someone drew
tracks of all the birds
he'd ever seen
and deer tracks,
lion tracks,
fox tracks . . .
even a wandering path
of the tracks of
men.

Men going where?
Searching for a
better place
for the tribe
to make its home?
Or for some newer
hunting ground?

Did pictures bring
strength
to the hunters?

Did they bring luck?
Was there some
magic
in the artist's hand?

There must have been magic
in songs and dances too...
Songs to protect
hunters,
songs to make
children grow
and corn grow
and pumpkins.

People danced.

You ALMOST know
how it must have been.
Long lines of dancers
move
into the shadows.

You ALMOST hear
the chanting
and the flute
and the rattles
and the drums
that called down rain
and made the night winds
blow.

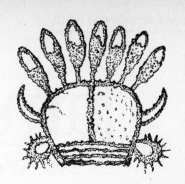

Sometimes
the dancers put on
masks.
Their artists drew
those great fierce faces
with headdresses
so tall and bright
and feathery
that they looked
part bird
part sky,
part mountain—
no longer men at all.

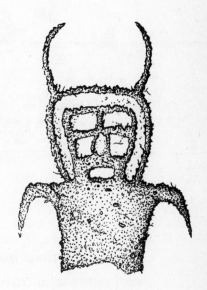

And
this canyon
echoed
with their voices.

Did they ever
wonder
who
in some far later time
would stand
in their
canyon
and think of them
and ALMOST hear
the echo of those voices
still in the wind?

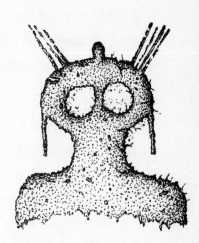

*Today you can see beautiful rock paintings of the Anasazi at Cliff Palace in Mesa Verde National Park in Colorado. Suppose you drew paintings to describe your life and your community. What pictures would you draw?*

Source: Byrd Baylor, *Before You Came This Way*. New York: Dutton, 1969.

# Jamestown
## New World Adventure

**by James E. Knight**

*These selections from a fictional but fact-based journal tell the story of a carpenter who traveled to America to help begin a new English colony. The world he found was new to him, but it was of course very familiar to the people who already lived there! The journal entries record the experiences and struggles of the original Jamestown colonists. What made life in Jamestown so difficult? What help did the colonists find?*

May 14, 1607

This journal will record the adventures of Israel Worth in the new colony of James Towne. At the time of this first entry, I am twenty-eight years old and in good health. I am one of four **master** carpenters on this **expedition**.

As I write, I am aboard the ship *Susan Constant*, with Captain Christopher Newport in command....

How sweet the land smells after our long voyage. From the ship I can see a white sandy beach and tall pines. The air is mild. The river beyond this bay looks broader than any I have seen in England. As with our colony, the river has been named James, after our King.

**master:** expert

**expedition:** journey made for a specific purpose

36

When we entered the **Bay of the Chesapeake**, a few days back, there was trouble. We were anchored off a point of land, which the Captain called Cape Henry. He and some of our men went ashore. They were attacked by Indians. Two sailors were wounded by arrows, and one of them died today.

Earlier today we carried men and goods to shore. Some of the men are now asleep in canvas shelters in the forest. I will go ashore tomorrow....

**Bay of the Chesapeake:** Chesapeake Bay

## June 7, 1607

For three weeks now, I have been ashore. We are clearing the land. From dawn to dusk we **labor** at cutting down trees.

**labor:** work

Despite our earlier troubles with the Indians, things had been going smoothly between us. We have seen them several times, and they have given us corn.

But yesterday, while some of our leaders were out exploring, trouble began. Some two hundred warriors attacked with spears and arrows. Many of us were wounded, and one boy was killed. We drove the Indians back with **musketfire**. They seemed terrified of it.

**musketfire:** shots from a gun with a long barrel

This has taught us a hard lesson. We must build a fort to protect ourselves. We will call it James Fort, and it will face the river. As a carpenter, I will be busy with this for some time. The fort will be made of upright logs, and it will be shaped like a triangle. Other buildings will be added later. **Bulwarks** will be **erected** at each corner of the fort. From these high towers, we will set up our **artillery**....

**bulwarks:** walls built for defense
**erected:** built
**artillery:** large, heavy weapons

## July 5, 1607

Sudden disease has struck our colony. Ten days ago we were in good health. Now men take to their beds, shaking with fever. They die—of what we often do not know. We bury them secretly at night. We are afraid that the Indians will learn how few we are.

Captain Smith is not surprised by the disease. He says that we should have dug freshwater wells. Instead, we have been drinking from the bay at low tide, when the water is least salty.

The Captain says this disease is caused by hot weather, hard work, and bad diet.

How strange that our food supplies should be low. We are on **half-rations** now. Yet, this land is not without plenty. Birds and fur-bearing animals fill the forest. Raccoons grow large as foxes. Crabs, mussels, oysters, and fish are plentiful. But we do not have the skills of the Indians. We cannot catch enough fish or hunt enough animals to feed ourselves....

**half-rations:** half portions

**February 28, 1608**

Much has happened. We shall not leave James Towne after all. Captain Smith's new friends among Powhatan's people have saved us. They come out of the forest often now. They bring fish, bread, corn, turkeys, and raccoons. Without them, we would never survive.

A young Indian maiden often leads the food-bearers. She is Pocahontas, daughter of King Powhatan and a Princess in this land. I cannot but think she is only eleven or twelve years of age. But she has shown herself to be a true friend....

**May 14, 1608**

James Towne is one year old today! It is longer than that since I have seen my home and family. My old friend, Angus Murchison, and I are sad. We are among the few "old men" in this place. There are but thirty-eight of us left from the original one hundred....

## December 10, 1608

For a week we have been splitting logs and loading them aboard the ship. Today it set sail for England. We must send something back to the Virginia Company in London—even if it is only wood for roofing. There is no gold to be found here.

Captain Smith has taken charge and has done much. The fort has been made larger and stronger. A storehouse and other buildings have been added. We have dug a well. . . .

## January 30, 1609

It is winter again, and a New Year. The colony has lasted through these cruel months only because of Captain Smith. When our food runs low, he goes to Powhatan. He gets corn and other goods from him. . . .

## August 12, 1609

Yesterday six ships anchored at James Towne! They were **battered** and weather-beaten. They are part of a large relief supply sent by the Virginia Company. Unfortunately, the flagship, the *Sea Venture*, was blown off course near Bermuda. Some fear the *Sea Venture*'s passengers are lost forever.

**battered:** damaged

The ships that did arrive brought three hundred new settlers. Surely we need them, but we have not so much as a roof to cover their heads. And they are ill-prepared for life here. How shall we feed them when winter comes? . . .

## September 3, 1609

Captain Smith has been injured. While he was out on the **barge**, his **powder bag** exploded. The men carried him back to the fort more dead than alive. We pray for his recovery.

**barge:** large boat
**powder bag:** bag with gunpowder in it

## October 3, 1609

Today, Captain Smith was taken aboard one of the ships. He must sail for England. He has no other choice. With his painful injuries, he cannot carry on. But how shall we survive without him?...

## November 16, 1609

Things are worse in James Towne, now that Captain Smith is gone. Food is scarce. Some of the new settlers have already died. Our leaders fight among themselves. No one leads.

There is no one to deal with Powhatan and his people. Our leaders are cruel to the Indians. So they turn against us. They bring no more food. They attack us in the forest. They know that Smith has gone. And Pocahontas comes no more....

## February 25, 1610

This is truly the starving time. I can hardly stand from weakness. When Captain Smith departed, there were five hundred of us. There are, I think, but one hundred left now.

For food today, I found some young hazel logs. I stripped away the green bark and chewed it for the juices.

My wife and daughter are much in my thoughts. God bless them and keep them. And God help me....

*These were the last words Israel Worth wrote in his journal. The next words were written on May 1, 1610, by his friend Angus Murchison. They say that Israel did not survive. "Two days after he last put his quill to paper, he left the fort with some others to search for food. They never returned." Angus also wrote that "James Towne could not have survived without men like Israel Worth." And, he wrote, "James Towne has survived."*

Source: James E. Knight, *Jamestown: New World Adventure*. Mahwah, NJ: Troll Associates, 1982.

# ...if you lived in Colonial Times

## by Ann McGovern

*Colonists knew that they had to work hard if they were to survive. They had few luxuries because they could not afford more. Picture a school with only one book. Think what it would be like if your classroom was heated by a fireplace. As you read the excerpted questions and answers from Ann McGovern's book, compare your home and school to those of the English colonists. What seems similar? What seems different?*

*Did children have to worry about table manners?*

...You could not say a word at the table. "Speak not" was a rule to remember. There were many rules to remember.

"Sing not, hum not, wriggle not" was one rule.

Has your mother ever said to you, "Don't take such big bites. Don't make so much noise when you chew"?

There were the same rules in colonial days. All the rules were printed in a book of manners, and you had to learn them all.

The book of manners said, "Stuff not thy mouth to fill thy cheeks.

"Make not a noise with thy tongue, lips, or breath in thy eating or drinking."...

### Did children go to school?

Some did. Some didn't.

The first school that boys and girls went to in colonial days was called a Dame School. The teacher was a woman, and the children came to her house. In Dame School, children learned to read and write.

### Who learned more—girls or boys?

After Dame School, boys went on to another school to learn more. Girls stayed home....

But some people said, "Girls are as clever as boys. Why can't they learn too?" So they taught their daughters at home.

Most boys had to go to school. The law said so. The law said every town with fifty families must build a school for boys. But some towns did not have enough money to build a school.

### What were the schools like?

The law did not say schools had to be comfortable. And most of them weren't.

There were hard benches to sit on.

The school had only one room, which was freezing cold in the winter.

The only heat came from the fireplace. Every boy had to bring firewood for the fire. If he forgot, he had to sit far away from the fire. He had to sit in the coldest part of the room.

The family of every boy who went to school had to pay the schoolmaster. Often he was paid in corn or other food.

Sometimes the schoolmaster had more food than he could eat. That happened once to a schoolmaster in the town of Salem. The schoolmaster had too much corn.

So he made one of the boys stand near an open window. When the boy saw someone walking by, he tried to trade the extra corn for something the schoolmaster could use.

There were no blackboards and no maps in colonial schools. There were no pencils, either. Boys wrote with a lump of lead. Or they wrote with a goose-quill pen dipped in homemade ink.

Paper was hard to get and cost a lot. Most boys wrote on birchbark. They could always get more in the woods. All they had to do was peel the bark off the birch trees.

Boys spent a lot of time learning to have nice handwriting. If they wrote their words clear and small, no one cared how the words were spelled. People spelled the same words in different ways. One schoolmaster put a notice in the paper to say that he taught "writing and spilling."

The *New England Primer* was the only schoolbook. It had many prayers. It had many questions and answers about God. And there were rhymes for each letter of the alphabet. For the letter D, the boys learned:

> A Dog will bite
> a thief at night.

As soon as the boys knew everything in the *New England Primer*, they could go to another school to learn more. Some boys were ready for college when they were only eleven years old. A few boys with rich fathers went to college in England.

But most boys stopped going to school. They went to work instead.

*Do you have more questions about colonial life? If you do, you can probably find answers by reading the rest of Ann McGovern's ... if you lived in* **Colonial Times.** *Look for the book in your school or local library.*

Source: Ann McGovern, *... if you lived in Colonial Times.* New York: Four Winds, 1964.

# In Good Old Colony Times

## American Ballad

*After the sun had set and the day's work was over, the Pilgrims often sang songs to entertain themselves. Many sang ballads, or songs that tell a story. These songs were passed along from town to town. Later they were written down and published. The ballad below was popular in the early days of our country. Why do the miller, the weaver, and the tailor fall into trouble?*

*Words adapted by Phyllis R. Kaplan*

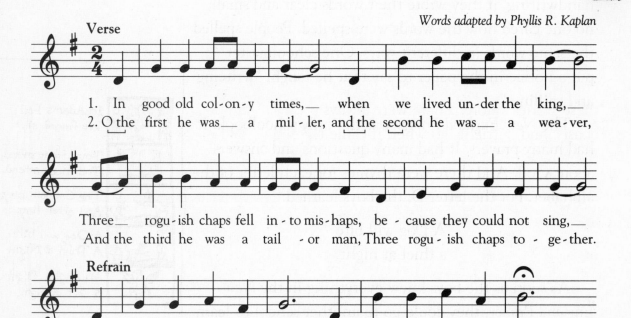

**Verse**

1. In good old col-on-y times,__ when we lived un-der the king,__
2. O the first he was__ a mil-ler, and the second he was__ a wea-ver,

Three__ rogu-ish chaps fell in-to mis-haps, be-cause they could not sing,__
And the third he was a tail-or man, Three rogu-ish chaps to-ge-ther.

**Refrain**

Be-cause they could not sing, Be-cause they could not sing,

Three__ rogu-ish chaps fell in-to mis-haps, be-cause they could not sing.

3. O the miller, he stole corn;
   and the weaver, he stole yarn,
   And the tailor man ran right away
   with the broadcloth under his arm.

4. The miller was drowned in the dam,
   and the weaver got hung in his yarn,
   And the tailor tripped as he ran away
   with the broadcloth under his arm.

# STRIKING IT RICH
## The Story of the California Gold Rush
### by Stephen Krensky

*Do you believe everything you hear? The discovery of gold in California in 1848 was spread by word of mouth at first. In this story the rumors were so tempting that the people of San Francisco deserted their town to search for gold in the hills. As you read the story, think about why they left. Would you have done the same?*

*GOLD!*

The news was big if it was true—but was it? San Francisco might be a sleepy little town, but it had heard these stories before. There were always plenty of rumors, boasts, and outright lies when it came to finding gold in the hills.

The facts behind this latest story were plain enough. They began with James Marshall, a carpenter. He was helping to build a sawmill on the American River, a hundred miles to the east.

Marshall had little education, but he had sharp eyes and was nobody's fool. On January 24, 1848, he was digging in the riverbed. There he spotted a glittering yellow rock, no bigger than his thumbnail.

Gold, thought Marshall, or maybe iron pyrite, which looks like gold but is more brittle. He struck the metal with a hammer. It flattened but did not break—a good sign. But Marshall was a busy man. He stuck the rock in his hat and went back to work.

Later, he rode to Sutter's Fort to see his boss, John A. Sutter. Born in Switzerland, Sutter had been a farmer, a trader, and a fur trapper. He had never been too successful.

Sutter and Marshall carefully examined the rock. They bit it to see if it was soft like gold. It was. They dabbed it with acid to see if its shine would dim. It didn't. Then they weighed it against silver and other things they knew were lighter than gold.

The rock passed every test. It was gold, all right.

Sutter told Marshall to keep the gold a secret. It might not amount to much, but it could still distract the men from their jobs.

But secrets like that don't last. Sutter's men soon learned what Marshall had found. On Sundays, their day off, they began to look for nuggets and gold dust. Some workers collected enough gold in an hour to equal a month's pay.

By the spring of 1848, more and more tales were reaching San Francisco, which was home to 800 people. Miners were **bragging** about scraping gold off rocks with their knives. Why, one fellow had hit a $50 nugget while digging a hole for his tent pole.

**bragging:** boasting

Didn't there have to be a little truth to these reports? Many people thought so, and the gold fever spread. Lawyers dropped their clients and soldiers **deserted** their posts. The schoolhouse closed after its only teacher ran off. Then the mayor disappeared. And nobody could complain to the sheriff because he was gone, too.

**deserted:** ran away from

By the end of June, San Francisco was almost a ghost town. Stores were empty. Doors blew open in the wind. Dogs roamed the streets and wooden sidewalks with only their shadows for company.

Everyone, it seemed, had left for the hills.

*Find out what happens when rumors are spread. Play the game "Whisper down the Alley," in which one person whispers a sentence to someone who then whispers it to someone else, and so on. Have the last person say out loud what he or she heard. How close to the original sentence is it?*

Source: Stephen Krensky, *Striking It Rich, The Story of the California Gold Rush*. New York: Simon & Schuster Books for Young Readers, 1996.

# Mr. Blue Jeans
## — A Story about Levi Strauss —
### by Maryann N. Weidt

*Levi Strauss came to the United States at the age of 18 with little money and without knowing English. Yet he went on to become famous throughout the country for his well-made blue jeans with copper rivets. Read this story of Levi's first pair of pants. What are some of the things he did that showed he would be successful someday?*

One sunny day, Levi was enjoying his lunch on the banks of the Sacramento River. A miner came by and asked Levi what he had for sale. Levi pulled a bolt of canvas out of his wagon and suggested that the **prospector** take a new tent to the diggings. The miner said that he didn't need a tent but could use some good, sturdy pants. Levi thought for a moment and then looked for a piece of string. Using a length of cording, he took the man's measurements. He told the fellow he would have a pair of long-wearing pants by sundown.

**prospector:** miner

Now Levi had to find a tailor to make the pants. It was not as easy as he thought it would be. Many of the tailors had gone to seek their fortunes in the mines. Finally Levi found one in a nearby town who had not been caught up by gold fever. Levi asked the man to make a pair of canvas pants in the miner's size and to sew the rest of the fabric into various other sizes.

That evening Levi found the prospector near the place he had left him and presented him with the pants. The miner could not believe his good luck. He grabbed the pants and pulled them on right over his ragged old trousers. The pants felt like they would last, and the miner **reckoned** that the pockets were big enough for his gold samples. He cheerfully paid Levi six dollars in gold dust.

**reckoned:** thought

Before long the miner had spread the word in the gold camps along the river about "those pants of Levi's." Soon Levi had sold all the pants he had ordered from the tailor.

Levi wrote to his brothers in New York and ordered additional canvas for more pants. The fabric they shipped, however, was not canvas but a heavy cotton material called denim. Made in the French town of Nimes, the cloth was named denim (for *de Nimes*) by the Americans. Pants made of this denim were popular with Genoese sailors and came to be nicknamed jeans after the Italian city of Genoa.

Within a few years, miners were not the only ones wearing Levi's pants. Overland traders carried the news of these new trousers to the Southwest and especially to Texas. Cowboys liked them because they lasted longer and were more comfortable to wear in the saddle than other pants. The men who came West to work on the railroad found that Levi's pants could withstand the long days they put in. Farmers wore them as well. They called the pants waist-high overalls, a name Levi himself preferred.

No one knows for sure if the story of Levi's first pair of pants is entirely accurate. The San Francisco earthquake of 1906 destroyed many of the Levi Strauss & Co.'s records. What is certain, however, is that by the 1860s, men everywhere were wearing "those pants of Levi's."

*Today Levi Strauss and Co. is the world's largest manufacturer of name-brand jeans. Each year the company uses almost 1.25 million miles of thread to make its jeans—enough to wrap around the world more than 50 times!*

Source: Maryann N. Weidt, *Mr. Blue Jeans, A Story about Levi Strauss.* Minneapolis: Carolrhoda Books, 1990.

# EARTHQUAKE!

## A STORY OF OLD SAN FRANCISCO

**by Kathleen V. Kudlinski**

*On April 18, 1906, San Francisco was hit by a powerful earthquake. In this story of historical fiction, Phillip tries to save his family's horses right after the earthquake. Everyday things that Phillip took for granted were no longer the same afterward. What are some of the things that were surprising and unexpected? What happened as a result of the earthquake?*

Phillip turned and reached to blow the lantern out—when the stable floor jerked under his feet. Another **quake**? Not again! he thought wildly. He grabbed for the nearest stall door, but it was already over. The horses danced in their stalls, snorting nervously. An **aftershock**, he told himself. Just an aftershock. He'd heard about them.

"Rest easy, fellas. The worst is over," he said. "Nothing to worry—"Another sharp shock nearly knocked him off his feet. It did knock the lantern off its peg.

**quake:** earthquake

**aftershock:** vibration after the initial earthquake

Phillip **lunged** across the stable, trying to catch the lantern before it fell. He was too late. It bounced once against the wooden floor and came to rest by a bale of hay. Fuel splashed out where the lantern hit. By the time Phillip got to it, a puddle of the **kerosene** fuel had leaked onto the floor. With a *whoosh*, the puddle burst into flame, and the flame scampered outward toward the dry hay. Toward Phillip. Toward the horses.

Phillip had dipped a bucket into the big water **trough** before he even knew what he was doing. They'd practiced this. Barn fire. The greatest horror of any **stablemaster**. Dry hay, dry straw, feed sacks, and old wood, plus well-oiled leather—and nothing to stop it all from burning to ashes, along with the horses trapped inside.

Phillip threw the bucketful of water toward the fire. Over and over he scooped, twisted, threw, and scooped again, until the blaze was all out.

He scattered the straw with the toe of his boot and sprinkled water on every inch of the floor. Steam and smoke and the sounds of frantic horses filled the stable.

But the fire was out. "That's all for today, fellas." Phillip laughed and wondered why he was laughing. He shook his head. "Quiet down, now. Easy." He paused beside every stall to rub the horses' faces, to calm them. "The worst that can happen has happened," he told them. "At least the worst I can think of."

He looked over the door at Duchess and bit his lip as she neighed a weak greeting from the floor. He wanted to run to the house, to see Mama. Why wasn't Papa back? Had something happened to Chester?

He hurried to the stable doorway, then froze. Everywhere he looked, something was broken. The neighbor's chimney had fallen across the sidewalk. Birdbaths and porch chairs were lying where they'd been

**lunged:** jumped suddenly

**kerosene:** oil for lamps

**trough:** long box for holding water for animals

**stablemaster:** person in charge of caring for horses

thrown by the earthquake. Shutters dangled in the wind, and broken windows glinted in the early morning sun. He could hear the sounds of babies crying, of dogs barking, and—strangely—of birds singing.

The porch of the minister's house across the street looked crooked somehow. As Phillip watched, it toppled forward with a great splintering crash. Dust and dirt flew from beneath it. Buster started barking **desperately**. Pastor Olson opened his door and stopped just before he fell into the ruins. He stood in the empty doorway in silence, staring at the space where his porch had been.

**desperately:** with little hope

This looks like a dream, Phillip thought. A bad one. Pastor Olson was wearing his pajamas and nightcap. His arms hung limp at his sides. Phillip had never seen him without a suit and starched collar. Now there he was in blue-and-white striped nightclothes, in full view of everyone in the street. A tassel hung from his nightcap. It swung in time with the slow shaking of his head.

Phillip wanted to wave—to say something—but what was there to say?

Bobby Hunt appeared in the doorway and threw his arms around the pastor. Bobby was crying. Crying! The Bobby Hunt who used words like *gad!* and *Jehoshaphat!* right in school. The Bobby Hunt who tied broken glass to his kite strings to cut off everybody else's kites in the sky. The Bobby Hunt who kicked the blind cocker spaniel when he thought nobody was looking.

Phillip looked down so he wouldn't have to watch Bobby Hunt cry. The trolley tracks in the road in front of him lay twisted and ripped from the pavement. How would the trolley cars get through? How could horses drive their **buggies** over the jagged metal? What would happen now?

**buggy:** carriage

What had happened at his own house? Phillip held his breath and stepped out to look next door. Home was

standing tall and straight. The chimneys were both still there. The front porch wasn't sagging, either, Phillip thought—not one bit. At least his own house was safe. He breathed deeply.

Where was Papa? Phillip wanted him to come right to the door like Pastor Olson did. He had to tell him about the fire. About the horses. About Duchess. He fought against the wish to run to his house. There was one more barn chore he had to do.

The water trough had to be filled again. "Never leave a stable dry," he quoted Papa to the horses as he walked past their stalls. After the lantern fire, he knew he would never forget that rule again.

He leaned over the empty trough and turned on the tap. No water came out. He turned the knob all the way and all the way back. Nothing. No gush. No trickle. Not even a gurgle way back in the pipes. There was no water.

In the silence, Phillip heard fire bells clanging all over San Francisco.

*The earthquake lasted only a minute but it caused a fire that burned for three days and destroyed the homes and stores of over 250,000 San Franciscans. Communities hadn't learned yet how to make earthquake-proof buildings and water supplies. What things in the story show that the earthquake was unexpected?*

Source: Kathleen V. Kudlinski, *Earthquake! A Story of Old San Francisco*. New York: Puffin Books, 1993.

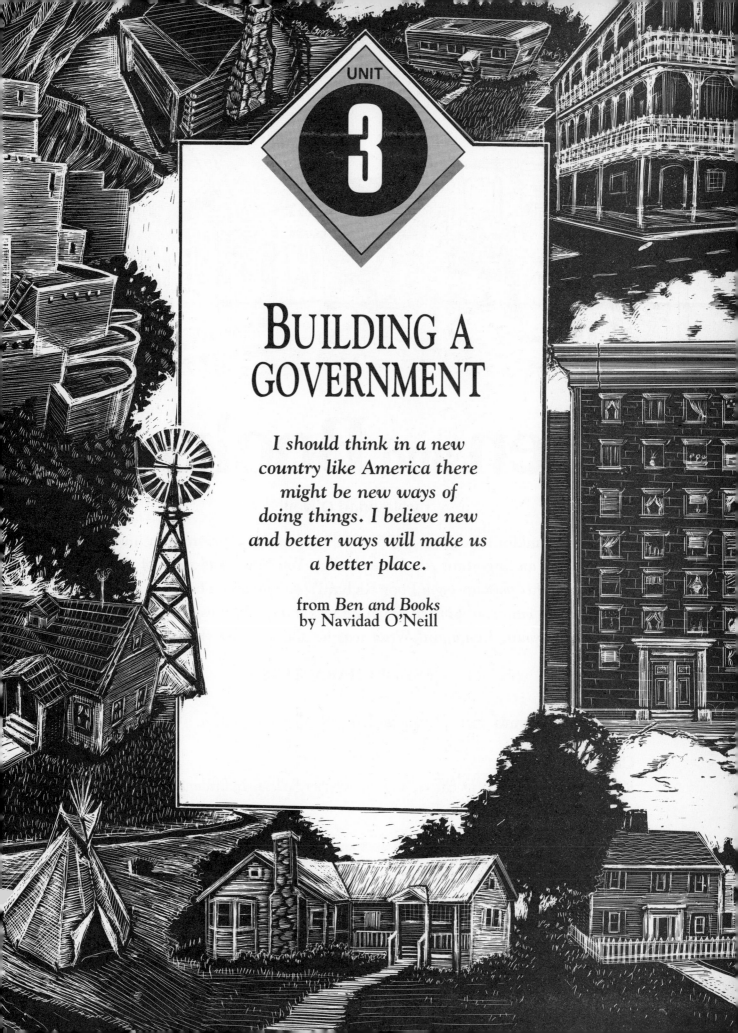

# BUILDING A GOVERNMENT

*I should think in a new
country like America there
might be new ways of
doing things. I believe new
and better ways will make us
a better place.*

from *Ben and Books*
by Navidad O'Neill

# Ben and Books

## by Navidad O'Neill

*Benjamin Franklin lived from 1706 to 1790. He was a printer, an inventor, a writer, and an important American leader. You have read some of the sayings from his popular book Poor Richard's Almanack. This play shows how Franklin educated himself when he was a boy. Why were books so important to young Benjamin? What was he able to learn from them?*

### CAST OF CHARACTERS

**Ben 1–6**
*Six boys and girls take turns playing the role of Benjamin Franklin.*

**Chorus**
*Kite Flyers, Swimmers, Debaters, and Newspaper Sellers. Individual students step out of chorus to become:*
**Debaters 1–4**
**Newspaper Seller 1**
**Newspaper Buyer**

*All six Benjamin Franklins stand behind one another in a line.*
*The first one in line speaks.*

**Ben 1:** To tell the story of Benjamin Franklin, it helps to have six Bens.

*Ben 1 steps out. Second Ben speaks.*

**Ben 2:** Benjamin Franklin helped found the country by signing the Declaration of Independence—but he also "found" many new ways of doing things.

*Ben 2 steps out. Third Ben speaks.*

**Ben 3:** He kept a diary, and he also wrote his life story in a book. His own words help us understand how he became such a great American.

*Ben 3 steps out. Fourth Ben speaks.*

**Ben 4:** We will tell you about only a few of the things he did, because if we told you everything he did, we would be here a long, long time.

*Ben 4 steps out. Fifth Ben speaks.*

**Ben 5:** Someday you should read Ben Franklin's autobiography for yourself and read about his life in his own words.

*Ben 5 steps out. Sixth Ben speaks.*

**Ben 6:** But now we will tell you what we know about the young boy named Ben.

*All the Bens scatter around the stage and sit while another Ben speaks. Ben 1 holds up a sign that says: THE ART OF THINKING. Sets it on chair. Stands beside it. The Kite Flyers hold kites and move them about the stage behind Ben 1 while he talks.*

**Ben 1:** A thought is like a kite…I think.
Kites are made of paper, string, and wood—nothing that flies on its own.
But put the ingredients together, and they fly.
I am a thinker.
I like to fly my thoughts just like a kite.
I think about one ordinary thing and another ordinary thing.
Then I keep them in my head and try to combine them into something new.
I like to see if together the things will fly.

**Ben 1:** When I was young, I read a book called *The Art of Thinking*.
I think thinking is one of the best things to think about.

*Ben 1 exits with Kite Flyers.*

*Ben 2 steps forward with a sign that reads:* THE ART OF SWIMMING.

**Ben 2:** I learned to swim from reading a book.
I grew up in Boston, which is on the Atlantic Ocean.
I loved to be near the sea.
I wanted to be a sailor when I grew up.
I thought swimming would be good to learn.
So I taught myself.
I read about the different strokes.

**Swimmers:** Back! (*They demonstrate the backstroke.*)

**Swimmers:** Side! (*They demonstrate the sidestroke.*)

**Swimmers:** Crawl! (*They demonstrate the crawl stroke.*)

**Swimmers:** Off!

*Ben 2 and Swimmers "swim off." Ben 3 steps forward with a sign that says:*
THE ART OF SPEAKING.

**Ben 3:** I love to argue.
I love to win arguments.
I spent a lot of time reading books which helped me win arguments.
They taught me how to use logic to win a debate.

I learned never to use words like "for sure" and "without a doubt it's true."
I never said I was 100 per cent certain. Instead I said, "If I am not
mistaken" and "I should think it is possible." I practice my new speaking
skills often.

*Debaters enter.*

**Ben 3:** I think girls should be educated just like boys.

**Debater 1:** Girls belong in the kitchen.

**Ben 3:** I should think that kitchen work could be done by boys and girls.

**Debater 2:** Girls are not as smart as boys. The education would be wasted.

**Ben 3:** If I'm not mistaken, girls are just as smart as boys. I've met girls who read and write and boys who read and write. While I have also met girls who do not care to read and write, I have also met boys who do not care to read and write.

**Debater 3:** So why bother if girls don't care to read and write?

**Ben 3:** I believe I said some do and some don't. Why not allow those who do the chance to learn.

**Debater 4:** Schooling is for males only. It always has been so, and it should always be so.

**Ben 3:** I should think in a new country like America there might be new ways of doing things. I believe new and better ways will make us a better place. If I'm not mistaken.

*Ben 3 and Debaters leave. Ben 4 and Ben 5 enter with a sign:*
THE ART OF WRITING.

**Ben 4:** I learned how to write the way I learned many things: by reading a book about it. I wanted to be a good writer, so I read good writing. When I found a sentence that I thought was beautiful, I would close the book. Then I would take out paper and my quill pen and try to write the sentence without looking. Then I would check back to see what mistakes I had made

**Ben 4:** and try again. Sometimes I would even improve the sentence. I wrote some sea songs that were especially hard because the words had to rhyme. All the time.
And when I sold the songs, I only made a dime.

**Ben 5:** But then I went to work for my brother who printed a newspaper. I would help set the big blocks of wood that printed the paper. I would stand at the corner and sell the newspaper.

*Chorus enters as Newspaper Sellers.*

**Newspaper Sellers:** Get your newspaper! *The New England Courant!* Best stories around! Get your newspaper!

**Ben 5:** I wanted to write for the paper, but my brother didn't think I was smart enough. So what I did was this: at night when everyone else was asleep, I wrote articles for the newspaper. I wrote them as if a woman were writing them. I named this woman "Silence Dogood." I wrote about how she thought the world should be. Then in the morning, before my brother arrived at the newspaper, I would slip the story under the door.

**Ben 4:** He read the stories by Silence Dogood and thought they were good enough to print in the paper.

**Ben 5:** He printed 14 in all.

**Newspaper Seller 1:** Get the *New England Courant!* New story by Silence Dogood.

**Newspaper Buyer:** I'll buy that paper. I like reading the stories of Silence Dogood. She is a fine writer. And it's nice to hear a woman's point of view for a change.

*Newspaper Sellers exit, still calling: "Buy your paper here!"*

*Ben 6 enters with a sign:* THE ART OF READING.

**Ben 6:** I read at an early age.
My sister says I was five.
All I know is I don't remember ever not reading.
Everything I learned, I learned from books.
Everything I accomplished when I was young was because of books.
Every story we've told you so far happened before I was 17 years old.
All because of books.

*Chorus and the other five Bens return with open books. A chorus member hands a book to Ben 6. He pretends to read from it:*

**Ben 6:** "When he was older, Benjamin Franklin created the first circulating library in the country. Now there are libraries everywhere. And in those libraries all across the country, you will find…"

**All:** "The Autobiography of Benjamin Franklin, 1706 to 1790."

*They shut their books.*

## THE END

*During the years of the American Revolution, Franklin spoke up for the colonies in Europe. Later he helped to arrange a peace between England and America. He was also one of the leaders who signed our Declaration of Independence. How did his ways of thinking as a child help him to succeed later in life?*

# Washington the Great

## Traditional American Song

*As a great general of the American Revolution and the first President of our country, George Washington holds a special place in American history. What are some of the qualities that made Washington a hero?*

*Traditional American Song*

**With Spirit**

1. I sup - pose you've heard of Wash - ing - ton,
2. And___ when King George of Eng - land
3. He___ was the first great Pres - i - dent,

Of Wash - ing - ton the Great,
Op - pressed their love - ly land,
The first to rule the land,

Who___ fought the French and In - di - ans
Our___ coun - try fought for free - dom then
And___ all the peo - ple hon - ored him

Up - on the north - ern lakes.
With Wash - ing - ton the Great.
Down to a sin - gle man.

Source: American Singer, Book 5, reprinted by permission of D.C. Heath & Co.

# ...If You Were There When They Signed the Constitution

**by Elizabeth Levy**

In 1787 leaders called delegates met in Philadelphia to write a plan of government for the new United States of America. This plan, called the Constitution, became the most important law of our country. What rules does the Constitution provide for choosing a President? Who makes the laws? What is the Bill of Rights? These are some of the questions you might have asked if you were there when the delegates signed the Constitution.

## How did the delegates invent a President?

The men at Philadelphia knew first hand what it was like to be ruled by a king. They wanted to make sure that no one man would ever have as much power as a king.

But on the other hand, they had lived for twelve years under a system when there was no head of the government, and that hadn't worked very well.

At the Philadelphia **Convention** during the hot summer, they had invented a House of Representatives and a Senate to make up the laws. But what if the House and the Senate voted foolish laws? Who would stop them? Would we have to go through another revolution?

No, they wanted a government where there would be someone strong enough to "check" the House and Senate, but not so strong that he could make himself king. They wanted someone who could lead the country in

**convention:** formal meeting for a certain purpose

times of emergency and deal with the heads of other nations. They decided to call this person "President."

### What does the President do?

The President cannot make laws. Only Congress can make laws, but the President has to carry out the laws. And the President can suggest laws.

One of the most important things any government has to decide is when and if to go to war. The delegates believed this was too big a question for one person to decide. It seemed to them that kings were always going to war and sending people to their deaths.

The delegates made the President Commander in Chief of the Army, but the President can not declare war on another country. Only Congress can declare war.

### Who would be President?

The truth was that everyone in the room knew exactly who would be the first President. They had been looking at him all summer. It was George Washington.

But they knew Washington wouldn't live forever. Remember, they were inventing a new office: President. Who should pick the President?

They went round and round on this question. First they voted that the President should be picked by the Senate, but then they didn't like that.

James Wilson from Philadelphia kept arguing that the President should be elected by the people as a whole. This was a lot for the delegates to swallow. It was rare for anyone in Georgia to know anyone in Massachusetts. How would anyone ever know who would be the best President?

In the end the delegates made up an "electoral college." Although the electoral college is a strange and **complicated** system, James Wilson was right. Almost from the beginning, the President came to be seen as not just from one state, but as someone who has to **represent** all the people.

**complicated:** not simple

**represent:** speak or act for

### Who would make the laws? Congress or the President?

It takes both Congress and the President to make a law. There are a lot of checks and balances built into the system.

Suppose a member of Congress suggests a law making everyone eat peanut butter and mayonnaise sandwiches for lunch every day.

"That's crazy!" you might say. But how would you stop the law?

The delegates wanted to make sure that before any suggestion became a law it would have to go through many steps, and at each step it could be "checked" or stopped if it was a bad law.

An awful lot of people would have to like peanut butter and mayonnaise before having it for lunch became the law.

### How are laws passed?

A law begins with a **proposal** called a *bill*. Most bills can start in either the House of Representatives or the Senate, but before a bill becomes a law, both branches of Congress must vote for it.

**proposal:** suggestion

Then the President gets the bill. If he or she doesn't like it, the President can say no, or veto it. (*Veto* comes from the Latin word "forbid.")

But the President's veto doesn't have to be the end of a bill. Congress can pass a bill over the President's veto if two-thirds of both the House and the Senate think the bill should be a law.

Chances are that two-thirds of the Senators and two-thirds of the Representatives would not like peanut butter and mayonnaise, and this bill would never get to be a law.

### Why did the delegates invent the Supreme Court?

The delegates knew that there would need to be a court to decide fights between the states, and to decide

if any of the states were passing laws that went against the Constitution. They had been using the British court system and expected their judges to go on following that tradition.

They knew that there would have to be a whole system of Federal Courts with a Supreme Court at the top, but they left out many details about how the courts would work.

The courts would be another check against any one group getting too much power. But how do you get an independent court?

The delegates decided to let the President **nominate** the Justices for the Supreme Court. However, the Senate would have to agree with the President's choice, or the President would have to suggest someone else.

**nominate:** choose for office

### How can we change the Constitution?

The delegates wanted their Constitution to last. They wanted people in the future to have a way to change the government without having another revolution.

They wanted their new Constitution to be easier to change than the old Articles of Confederation, which had said that nothing could be changed unless every single state agreed.

The Constitution spells out two ways it can be changed. One way would be to make major changes and to call another convention. It would take two-thirds of the states to call one.

This method has never been used.

The second way is to amend the Constitution.

### What is an amendment?

An amendment is a specific change in the Constitution. There have been amendments to end slavery and to give women the vote. All in all we have approved only twenty-six amendments.

It is not easy to change the Constitution with an amendment. An amendment has to be approved by

two-thirds of both the Senate and the House of Representatives.

Then it is taken to the states, where it has to be voted on by either the state legislature or a special convention. Three-quarters of all the states must pass an amendment before it becomes part of the Constitution.

### What was missing from the Constitution?

There was no Bill of Rights in the original Constitution. A Bill of Rights protects you, the individual, from the power of your government. The idea of a Bill of Rights, a list of things that the government cannot do, goes way back in English history, back to 1215, when the English lords made King John sign the **Magna Carta**.

**Magna Carta:** "Great Charter" listing rights that landowners and church leaders demanded from King John

### What are some of the rights in a Bill of Rights?

One of the rights guaranteed in a Bill of Rights is freedom of religion. Under English rule many colonists did not enjoy freedom to **worship** as they pleased. When James Madison was a young man in Virginia, the Church of England was the colony's official church. Baptists and Methodists were often thrown into jail.

**worship:** pray to God

After the Revolution, the state government of Virginia declared that all people should be free to worship as they choose. They made freedom of religion part of their Bill of Rights. The Virginia Bill of Rights also said that all men were free and equal. It forbade cruel and unusual punishment. It gave all people the right to trial by jury.

Many other states copied the Virginia Bill of Rights into their own Constitutions.

*The Bill of Rights was added to the Constitution in 1791 as the first ten amendments. These rights protect certain freedoms of Americans, such as the right to say what you want, go where you want, and practice whatever religion you want. The Constitution is more than 200 years old. Many say that it has lasted so long because amendments allow it to change with the times.*

Source: Elizabeth Levy, ...*If You Were There When They Signed the Constitution*. New York: Scholastic, 1987.

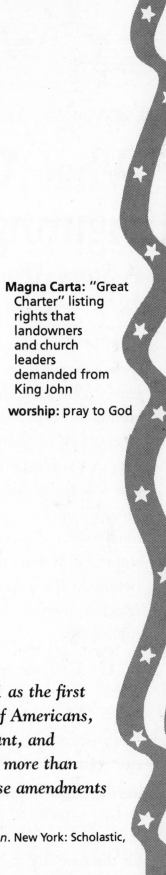

# What Are You Figuring Now?

## A Story About *Benjamin Banneker*

### by Jeri Ferris

*In 1731 Benjamin Banneker was born on a farm in Maryland. While most of the other African Americans on the farm were enslaved, Benjamin and his family were free. He grew up to become a good farmer, but he wanted to do even more. Banneker had a head for numbers. He studied as much math as he could on his own. Then in 1771 he became friends with George Ellicott, who was studying to be a surveyor, a person who measures land. Banneker was able to use his math knowledge to help his friend survey, and to learn this skill at the same time. With Ellicott's books and instruments, Banneker taught himself astronomy, too. He spent years studying the sun, moon, stars, and planets through his telescope. When he was almost 60 years old, Benjamin Banneker got the chance to use what he had learned. Read the selection from the biography below to see how he helped to build the new capital city.*

By 1790, the revolutionary war had been over for 7 years and the Declaration of Independence was 14 years old, but the new United States still had no capital. So President George Washington chose a spot for the city right in the middle of the 13 states, in the woods overlooking the Potomac River. He chose Frenchman Pierre L'Enfant to plan just where the streets and buildings would look best, and he ordered the survey for the new city to begin in 1791.

The surveyor had to lay out the straight lines for the 10-square-mile city. He had to **plot** a perfect line running north and south using the stars, his instruments, his **astronomical clock**, and his **calculations**. Then he had to cross it with a perfect line running east and west. The United States Capitol was to be built on the hill where the two lines crossed.

**plot:** make a map of

**astronomical clock:** a clock that shows the position of stars in the sky

**calculations:** figures arrived at by doing math

Major Andrew Ellicott, George Ellicott's cousin, was chosen to be the chief surveyor. But Major Ellicott needed help. He needed someone who knew astronomy and surveying. He needed someone who knew math and figuring. He needed someone who knew clocks. In short, he needed Benjamin Banneker.

President Washington and Thomas Jefferson, the secretary of state, agreed that Benjamin Banneker was just the man to be the chief surveyor's chief assistant. Benjamin hoped to prove they were right.

He put aside his telescope and **drafting** tools, and he packed his best dark suit and white linen shirts. He added his quill pen, an ink bottle, and some paper, in case he had time to make notes for his **almanac**. Before he left, he asked his sisters and their husbands to look after his farm.

**drafting:** drawing or sketching

**almanac:** a book put out every year, with information about the weather and many other subjects

On a cold, rainy morning in early February 1791, when Benjamin was almost 60 years old, he and Major Ellicott set off on horseback to make camp in Alexandria, Virginia, about 40 miles away. They arrived, wet and cold, on the evening of February 7.

The next day, the two men rode to a hill outside
the town to set up the **observation tent**, where
Benjamin would work. Andrew Ellicott owned some of
the finest astronomical instruments in the world, and
Benjamin was to use them. He was in charge of the
astronomical clock, three large telescopes, and many
other tools used in surveying.

At last the survey began. Andrew took his crew of
men and began chopping down trees so he could lay
out straight lines for the city. Benjamin set up the
largest and best telescope so that it pointed through an
opening in the roof of the tent. That night, he began
his observations of the stars as they crossed a certain
point in the sky. He recorded each observation,...

**observation tent: a
place from which to
watch things**

and drew the **base points** for the lines Andrew would lay the following day.

When the stars faded, Benjamin had time for only a short nap. Soon he was up again to explain his figures to Andrew, to record observations of the sun, and to check the astronomical clock.

It rained a lot that spring, and it was cold at night in the tent. In fact, it was cold in the daytime, too, but Benjamin was too busy to mind. If he ever had a spare minute, which wasn't often, he would use the time to work on his almanac.

On March 12, Benjamin's name was in the newspaper. The *Georgetown Weekly Ledger* reported that Andrew Ellicott was "attended by *Benjamin Banniker* . . .surveyor and astronomer." His name was spelled wrong again, but Benjamin carefully and proudly folded his copy of the newspaper and laid it aside with his notes.

That same month, Benjamin met the most famous man in the United States. President Washington himself came to visit the survey camp on March 28. Benjamin dressed in his best dark suit, his finest linen shirt, and a new three-cornered hat. He smiled when he heard someone in the crowd say that Mr. Banneker looked like Benjamin Franklin with brown skin.

When Benjamin bowed deeply before the tall president, he tried to feel as calm on the inside as he looked on the outside, but his heart felt like a runaway clock.

On April 15, Benjamin again dressed in his very best clothes. He stood with Andrew Ellicott and Pierre

L'Enfant as the first stone marker was placed at Jones's Point. This marked the first corner of the capital city.

By late spring, Benjamin had finished his figures. After working night and day, seven days a week, he was ready to return to his farm. Before he left, Benjamin looked at L'Enfant's plans for the new city. They showed streets laid out like a checkerboard, with wide avenues spreading out from the Capitol like the spokes of a wheel. They also included plenty of parks and fountains. Benjamin thought the plans were just right.

As he walked to his horse, Benjamin thought about his three months as the chief surveyor's chief assistant. He felt proud that he, Benjamin Banneker, had helped to lay out the capital city of the United States.

Benjamin stopped at the Ellicott's store on the way home to buy candles, ink, and paper. His neighbors saw him and hurried over to shake his hand and ask about his adventures.

Hours later, Benjamin shook the last hand and got back on his horse. In his bulging saddlebags were his suit, his notes, the newspaper with his name in it, and the new candles and ink from the store. Tucked away carefully was a brand-new, handsome book with three hundred blank pages of handmade paper. Benjamin planned to write his almanac on these fine pages.

At last he was home. When Benjamin opened the cabin door, he was greeted by the ticking of his wooden clock. The cabin was clean and neat. His sisters had taken good care of it and of his farm while he was gone.

*Later, Pierre L'Enfant had an argument with the city planners. He left the project and took the plans with him. Fortunately, Banneker was not only a good planner—he had a good memory as well! Banneker went on to help build Washington, D.C., which is still our capital today.*

Source: Jeri Ferris, *What Are You Figuring Now? A Story About Benjamin Banneker*. Minneapolis: Carolrhoda Books, 1988.

# City Green

### by DyAnne DiSalvo-Ryan

*Citizens can work together to bring change to their communities. Sometimes
people have to work for a long time to get what they need for their
neighborhoods. Sometimes they just need to know the right steps to follow.
In this story a young girl and her older friend come up with a plan to turn
an abandoned lot into a community garden. What steps do they they take
to achieve their goal?*

There used to be a building right here on this lot. It
was three floors up and down, an empty building nailed
up shut for as long as I could remember. My friend Miss
Rosa told me Old Man Hammer used to live there—
some other neighbors too. But when I asked him about
that, he only hollered, "Scram."

Old Man Hammer, hard as nails.

Last year two people from the city came by, dressed
in suits and holding papers. They said, "This building is
unsafe. It will have to be torn down."

By winter a crane with a wrecking ball was parked outside. Mama gathered everyone to watch from our front window. In three slow blows that building was knocked into a heap of pieces. Then workers took the **rubble** away in a truck and filled the hole with dirt.

rubble: rough, broken pieces of rock or other material

Now this block looks like a big smile with one tooth missing. Old Man Hammer sits on his stoop and shakes his head. "Look at that piece of junk land on a city block," Old Man Hammer says. "Once that building could've been saved. But nobody even tried."

And every day when I pass this lot it makes me sad to see it. Every single day.

Then spring comes, and right on schedule Miss Rosa starts cleaning her coffee cans. Miss Rosa and I keep coffee cans outside our windowsills. Every year we buy two packets of seeds at the hardware store—sometimes **marigolds**, sometimes **zinnias**, and one time we tried tomatoes. We go to the park, scoop some dirt, and fill up the cans halfway.

marigolds, zinnias: garden plants with colorful flowers

This time Old Man Hammer stops us on the way to the park. "This good for nothin' lot has plenty of dirt right here," he says.

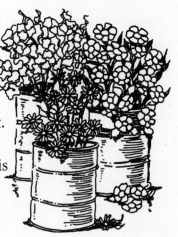

Then all at once I look at Miss Rosa. And she is smiling back at me. "A *lot* of dirt," Miss Rosa says.

"Like one big coffee can," I say.

That's when we decide to do something about this lot.

Quick as a wink I'm digging away, already thinking of gardens and flowers. But Old Man Hammer shakes his finger. "You can't dig more dirt than that. This lot is city property."

Miss Rosa and I go to see Mr. Bennett. He used to work for the city. "I seem to remember a program," he says, "that lets people rent empty lots."

That's how Miss Rosa and I form a group of people from our block. We pass around a **petition** that says: WE WANT TO LEASE THIS LOT. In less than a week we have plenty of names.

petition: formal request

"Sign with us?" I ask Old Man Hammer.

"I'm not signin' nothin'," he says. "And nothin' is what's gonna happen."

But something did.

The next week, a bunch of us take a bus to city hall. We walk up the steps to the proper office and hand the woman our list. She checks her files and types some notes and makes some copies. "That will be one dollar, please."

We rent the lot from the city that day. It was just as simple as that.

Saturday morning I'm up with the sun and looking at this lot. My mama looks out too. "Marcy," she says, and hugs me close. "Today I'm helping you and Rosa."

After shopping, Mama empties her grocery bags and folds them flat to carry under her arm. "Come on, Mrs. B.," Mama tells her friend. "We're going to clear this lot."

Then what do you know but my brother comes along. My brother is tall and strong. At first, he scratches his neck and shakes his head just like Old Man Hammer. But Mama smiles and says, "None of that here!" So all day long he piles junk in those bags and carries them to the curb.

Now, this time of day is early. Neighbors pass by and see what we're doing. Most say, "We want to help too." They have a little time to spare. Then this one calls that one and that one calls another.

"Come on and help," I call to Old Man Hammer.

"I'm not helpin' nobody," he hollers. "You're all wastin' your time."

**Sour grapes** my mama'd say, and sour grapes is right.

**sour grapes:** jealous

Just before supper, when we are good and hungry, my mama looks around this lot. "Marcy," she says, "you're making something happen here."

Next day the city drops off tools like rakes and brooms, and a **Dumpster** for trash. Now there's even more neighbors to help. Miss Rosa, my brother, and I say "Good morning" to Old Man Hammer, but Old Man Hammer just waves like he's swatting a fly.

**Dumpster:** brand name of large trash can

"Why is Old Man Hammer so mean and cranky these days?" my brother asks.

"Maybe he's really sad," I tell him. "Maybe he misses his building."

"That rotten old building?" My brother shrugs. "He should be happy the city tore down that mess."

"Give him time," Miss Rosa says. "Good things take time."

Mr. Bennett brings wood—old slats he's saved— and nails in a cup. "I knew all along I saved them for something," he says. "This wood's good wood."

Then Mr. Rocco from two houses down comes, carrying two cans of paint. "I'll never use these," he says. "The color's too bright. But here, this lot could use some brightening up."

Well, anyone can tell with all the excitement that something is going on. And everyone has an idea about what to plant—strawberries, carrots, lettuce, and more. Tulips and daisies, petunias, and more! Sonny turns the dirt over with a snow shovel. Even Leslie's baby tries to dig with a spoon.

For lunch, Miss Rosa brings milk and jelly and bread and spreads a beach towel where the junk is cleared. By the end of the day a fence is built and painted as bright as the sun.

Later, Mama kisses my cheek and closes my bedroom door. By the streetlights I see Old Man Hammer come down his steps to open the gate and walk to the back of this lot. He bends down quick, sprinkling something from his pocket and covering it over with dirt.

In the morning I tell my brother. "Oh, Marcy," he says. "You're dreaming. You're wishing too hard."

But I know what I saw, and I tell my mama, "Old Man Hammer's planted some seeds."

Right after breakfast, I walk to the back of this lot. And there it is—a tiny raised bed of soil. It is neat and tidy, just like the rows we've planted. Now I know for sure that Old Man Hammer planted something. So I pat the soil for good luck and make a little fence to keep the seeds safe.

Every day I go for a look inside our garden lot. Other neighbors stop in too. One day Mrs. Wells comes by. "This is right where my grandmother's bedroom used to be," she says. "That's why I planted my flowers there."

I feel sad when I hear that. With all the digging and planting and weeding and watering, I'd forgotten about the building that had been on this lot. Old Man Hammer had lived there too. I go to the back, where he planted his seeds. I wonder if this was the place where his room used to be.

I look down. Beside my feet, some tiny stems are sprouting. Old Man Hammer's seeds have grown! I run to his stoop. "Come with me!" I beg, tugging at his hand. "You'll want to see."

I walk him past the hollyhocks, the daisies, the peppers, the rows of lettuce. I show him the strawberries that I planted. When Old Man Hammer sees his little garden bed, his sour grapes turn sweet. "Marcy, child." He shakes his head. "This lot was good for nothin'. Now it's nothin' but good," he says.

Soon summertime comes, and this lot really grows. It fills with vegetables, herbs, and flowers. And way in the back, taller than anything else, is a beautiful patch of yellow sunflowers. Old Man Hammer comes every day. He sits in the sun, eats his lunch, and sometimes comes back with supper.

Nobody knows how the sunflowers came—not Leslie, my brother, or Miss Rosa. Not Mr. Bennett, or Sonny, or anyone else. But Old Man Hammer just sits there smiling at me. We know whose flowers they are.

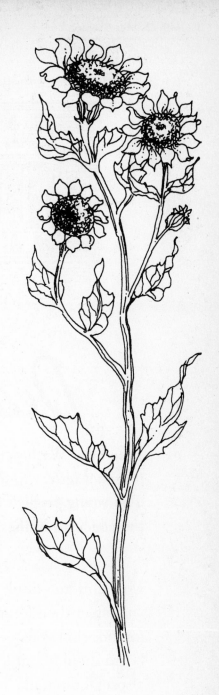

*All over the country people have started community gardens like Marcy and her neighbors did in this story. If you want to find out about the community gardening program that is closest to you, write to: American Community Gardening Association, 325 Walnut Street, Philadelphia, PA 19106.*

Source: DyAnne DiSalvo-Ryan, *City Green*. New York: William Morrow, 1994.

# Dear Mr. President

*When the Washington Post newspaper invited America's children to write personal letters to the nation's President, nearly 11,000 children wrote in. The young people's letters told of their hopes and fears. What are some of the concerns of these children? Which ideas do you think are good ones?*

I suggest a board of children that could advise you in what children think is important since your decisions will affect their future. You could have an election just for kids (kid voters). The kids that want to be on the board should be at least eight or nine. There could be a special room in a building for members to meet and discuss issues. There could be a representative from each state or county.

—*Sarah Troxel, age 9*

Why don't we build more houses for the poor people? We could sell some of my baseball cards to get money to get the bricks for the houses. I picked out some cards to sell.

—*Chris Field, age 6*

Most people look up to the president as a role model. If all of the prejudiced people in the world see that you believe that all people are created equal, they just may change their beliefs about people.

—*Sherese Melton, age 13*

I hope to see peace. Peace in this country and in our world. But peace is not easy to get. But one way to get it is listen, do not talk but listen. You can learn more things from listening than talking. Then, when you talk you will know more and maybe you will have peace with someone.

—*Chris Matthews, age 10*

I went to Colorado for twenty-one days to visit my Grandma. I rode an airplane for the second time. I went to the zoo and I read the signs and I learned some things that I did not know. I went in the tall mountains and I thought they were beautiful. I think America is a beautiful place to live. I hope it becomes safer.

—*Royce Lee Weeks-Jamieson, age 8*

You have a hard, hard job. You have to protect the world and if there is anything you need, call me. I'll be home.

—*Christopher Jennings, age 9*

I hope I can be like you. I haven't told anyone but that is my dream. I want to be a hero.

—*Devon Artusio, age 8*

**As one young writer said, "Although I am too young to drive [and] too young to vote . . . there is something I am old enough to do: give advice." What advice would you give the President?**

Source: Washington Post Co., *Dear President*. New York: Avon Books, 1993.

# Julio in the Lion's Den

## by Johanna Hurwitz

*You know that people vote in an election to choose government leaders to run their community. Students can also vote in an election to choose someone to lead their class. In the book Class President, Mr. Flores's fifth-grade class decides to hold an election to choose a class president. Julio Sanchez secretly wants to run, but he instead supports his best friend, Lucas. Lucas is running against Cricket Kaufman, the most popular girl in the class. Then, one day, Arthur Lewis breaks his glasses playing soccer. What does this have to do with the election? How does Julio find out what kind of president Cricket or Lucas would make?*

**O**n Monday, Arthur came to school with new glasses. Cricket came to class with a big poster that said, VOTE FOR CRICKET, THAT'S THE TICKET.

The election was going to be held on Friday. That meant there were only four days more to get ready. In the meantime, they learned about how to make a **nomination** and how to **second it**. It was going to be a really serious election.

At lunch, Cricket took out a bag of miniature chocolate bars and gave them out to her classmates.

**nomination:**
suggestion of a candidate, or someone who is running for office

**second it:** support it

Julio took his and ate it. But it didn't mean he was going to vote for Cricket. He wondered if there was anything Lucas could give out that was better than chocolate. Nothing was better than chocolate!

"If you're going to run against Cricket, we've got to get to work," Julio told Lucas on their way home. Julio wasn't very good at making posters, as Cricket and Zoe were, but he was determined to help his friend.

The next morning, a new poster appeared in Mr. Flores's classroom. It said, DON'T BUG ME. VOTE FOR LUCAS COTT. Julio had made it.

Before lunch, Mr. Flores read an announcement from the principal. "From now on, there is to be no more soccer playing in the school yard at lunchtime."

"No more soccer playing?" Julio called out. "Why not?"

Mr. Flores looked at Julio. "If you give me a moment, I'll explain. Mr. Herbertson is concerned about accidents. Last week, Arthur broke his glasses. Another time, someone might be injured more seriously."

Julio was about to call out again, but he remembered just in time and raised his hand.

"Yes, Julio," said Mr. Flores.

"It's not fair to make us stop playing soccer just because someone *might* get hurt. Someone might fall down walking to school, but we still have to come to school every day."

Julio didn't mean to be funny, but everyone started to laugh. Even Mr. Flores smiled.

"There must be other activities to keep you fellows busy at lunchtime," he said. "Is soccer the only thing you can do?"

Lucas raised his hand. "I don't like jumping rope," he said when the teacher called on him.

All the girls giggled at that.

"You could play jacks," suggested Cricket. Everyone knew it wasn't a serious possibility, though.

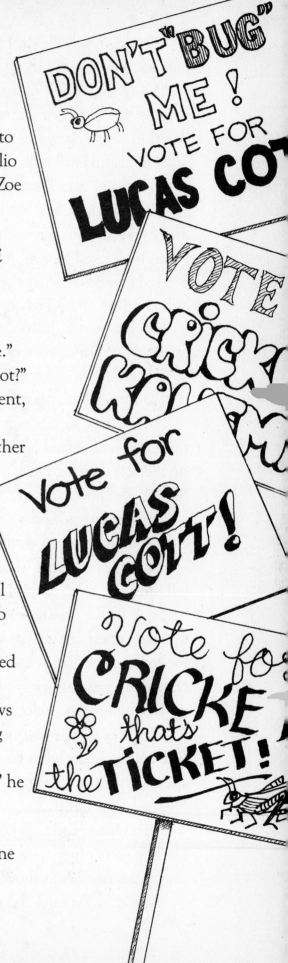

"Couldn't we tell Mr. Herbertson that we want to play soccer?" asked Julio.

"You could make an **appointment** to speak to him, if you'd like," said Mr. Flores. "He might change his decision if you convince him that you are right."

appointment: date to meet or see someone

"Lucas and I will talk to him," said Julio. "Right, Lucas?"

"Uh, sure," said Lucas, but he didn't look too sure.

The principal, Mr. Herbertson, spoke in a loud voice and had eyes that seemed to bore right into your head when he looked at you. Julio had been a little bit afraid of Mr. Herbertson since the very first day of kindergarten. Why had he offered to go to his office and talk to him?

Mr. Flores sent Julio and Lucas down to the principal's office with a note, but the principal was out of the office at a meeting.

"You can talk to him at one o'clock," the secretary said.

At lunch, Cricket had more chocolate bars. This time, she had pasted labels on them and printed in tiny letters, *Cricket is the ticket*. She must be spending her whole allowance on the **campaign**, Julio thought.

After a few more days of free chocolate bars, everyone in the class would be voting for Cricket.

campaign: time before an election when candidates try to win votes

At recess, the girls were jumping rope. You could fall jumping rope, too, Julio thought.

Back in the classroom, Julio wished he could think up some good arguments to tell the principal. He looked over at Lucas. Lucas didn't look very good. Maybe he was coming down with the flu.

Just before one o'clock, Julio had a great idea. Cricket was always saying she wanted to be a lawyer. She always knew what to say in class. Julio figured she'd know just what to do in the principal's office, too. He raised his hand.

"Mr. Flores, can Cricket go down to Mr. Herbertson's office with Lucas and me? She's running for president, so she should stick up for our class."

"Me?" Cricket said. "I don't care if we can't play soccer."

"Of course," teased Lucas. "You couldn't kick a ball if it was glued to your foot."

"Cricket," said Mr. Flores, "even if you don't want to play soccer, others in the class do. If you are elected, you will be president of the whole class, not just the girls. I think going to the meeting with Mr. Herbertson will be a good **opportunity** for you to **represent** the class."

**opportunity:** chance
**represent:** speak for

So that was why at one o'clock Julio, Lucas, and Cricket Kaufman went downstairs to the principal's office.

Mr. Herbertson **gestured** for them to sit in the chairs facing his desk. Cricket looked as pale as Lucas. Maybe she, too, was coming down with the flu.

**gestured:** showed with hands

Julio waited for the future first woman President of the United States to say something, but Cricket didn't say a word. Neither did Lucas. Julio didn't know what to do. They couldn't just sit here and say nothing.

Julio took a deep breath. If Cricket or Lucas wasn't going to talk, he would have to do it. Julio started right in.

"We came to tell you that it isn't fair that no one can play soccer at recess just because Arthur Lewis broke his eyeglasses. Anybody can have an accident. He could have tripped and broken them getting on the school bus." Julio was amazed that so many words had managed to get out of his mouth. No one else said anything, so he went on. "Besides, a girl could fall jumping rope," said Julio. "But you didn't say that they had to stop jumping rope."

"I hadn't thought of that," said Mr. Herbertson.

Cricket looked alarmed. "Can't we jump rope anymore?" she asked.

"I didn't mean that you should make the girls stop jumping rope," Julio went on quickly. He stopped to think of a better example. "Your chair could break while you're sitting on it, Mr. Herbertson," he said.

Mr. Herbertson adjusted himself in his chair. "I certainly hope not," he said, smiling. "What is your name, young man?"

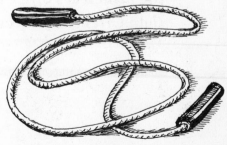

"Julio. Julio Sanchez." He pronounced it in the Spanish way with the J having an H sound.

"You have a couple of brothers who also attended this school, Julio, don't you?" asked the principal. "Nice fellows. I remember them both."

Julio smiled. He didn't know why he had always been afraid of the principal. He was just like any other person.

"Julio," Mr. Herbertson went on, "you've got a good head on your shoulders, just like your brothers. You made some very good points this afternoon. I think I can arrange things so that there will be more teachers **supervising** the yard during recess. Then you fellows can play soccer again tomorrow." He turned to Cricket. "You can jump rope if you'd rather do that," he said.

**supervising:** watching over

Cricket smiled. She didn't look so pale anymore.

Julio and Lucas and Cricket returned to Mr. Flores's classroom. "It's all arranged," said Cricket as soon as they walked in the door.

The class burst into cheers.

"Good work," said Mr. Flores.

Julio was proud that he had stood up to Mr. Herbertson. However, it wasn't fair that Cricket made it seem as if she had done all the work. She had hardly done a thing. For that matter, Lucas hadn't said anything, either. For a moment, Julio wished he hadn't offered to be Lucas's campaign **manager**. He wished he was the one running for class president. He knew he could be a good leader.

**manager:** person in charge

*Do you think Julio would make a good leader? Why? What happened in the principal's office that showed he might be a better class president than Cricket or Lucas? What qualities should a class president have?*

Source: Johanna Hurwitz, *Class President*. New York: Scholastic, 1990.

# COMMUNITIES ON THE MOVE

*Everybody says it was
something to see how fast
that town grew. All those
people moving in and
houses going up.*

Pattie Frances Ridley Jones
in *Childtimes*

# DIARY OF
# MRS. AMELIA STEWART KNIGHT

## AN OREGON PIONEER OF 1853

**by Amelia Stewart Knight**

*From the 1840s to the 1870s, settlers followed the Oregon Trail westward to the Oregon territory. The journey took about six months by wagon train. This selection from Amelia Stewart Knight's diary describes some of the difficulties of the overland trip. What made travel by wagon so hard? Why do you think Mrs. Knight noted so many details about the weather?*

*Saturday, April 9, 1853.* STARTED FROM HOME about 11 o'clock and traveled 8 miles and camped in an old house; night cold and frosty.

*Thursday, April 14th.* Quite cold. Little **ewes** crying with cold feet. Sixteen wagons all getting ready to cross the creek. **Hurrah** and **bustle** to get breakfast over. Feed the cattle. Hurrah boys, all ready, we will be the first to cross the creek this morning. Gee up Tip and Tyler, and away we go the sun just rising.

**ewes:** female sheep

**hurrah:** hurry
**bustle:** stir, excited activity

*Wednesday, April 20th*. Cloudy. We are creeping along slowly, one wagon after another, the same old **gait**; and the same thing over, out of one mud hole into another all day. Crossed a branch where the water run into the wagons. No corn to be had within 75 miles. Came 18 miles and camp.

**gait:** pace

*Friday, April 22nd*. Still bad weather. no sun; traveling on, mile after mile in the mud, mud....

*Saturday, April 30th*. Fine weather; spent this day in washing, baking, and overhauling the wagons. Several more wagons have camped around us.

*Sunday, May 1st*. Still fine weather; wash and scrub all the children.

*Saturday, May 7th*....No wood, only enough to boil some coffee. Good grass for the **stock**. We have crossed a small creek, with a narrow Indian bridge across it. Paid the Indians 75 cents toll. My hands are numb with cold....

**stock:** animals

*Sunday, May 8th*. Still in camp. Waiting to cross [the Elkhorn River]. There are three hundred or more wagons in sight and as far as the eye can reach, the bottom is covered, on each side of the river, with cattle and horses. There is no ferry here and the men will have to make one out of the tightest wagon-bed (every company should have a waterproof wagon-bed for this purpose). Everything must now be hauled out of the wagons head over heels (and he who knows where to find anything will be a smart fellow) then the wagons must be all taken to pieces, and then by means of a strong rope stretched across the river with a tight wagon-bed attached to the middle of it, the rope must be long enough to pull from one side to the other, with men on each side of the river to pull it. In this way we have to cross everything a little at a time....

*Friday, May 13th.* It is thundering and bids fair for rain. Crossed the river early this morning before breakfast. (Got breakfast over after a fashion. Sand all around ankle deep; wind blowing; no matter, hurry it over. Them that eat the most breakfast eat the most sand.)...

*Monday, May 16th.* Evening—We have had all kinds of weather today. This morning was dry, dusty and sandy. This afternoon it rained, hailed, and the wind was very high. Have been traveling all the afternoon in mud and water up to our **hubs**. Broke chains and stuck in the mud several times.

**hubs:** centers of wheels

*Tuesday, May 31st.* Evening—Traveled 25 miles today. When we started this morning there were two large **droves** of cattle and about 50 wagons ahead of us, and we either had to stay poking behind them in the dust or hurry up and drive past them. It was no fool of a job to be mixed up with several hundred head of cattle, and only one road to travel in, and the drivers threatening to drive their cattle over you if you attempted to pass them.

**droves:** groups of animals

*Wednesday, June 1st.* It has been raining all day long and we have been traveling in it so as to be able to keep ahead of the large droves. The men and boys are all soaking wet and look sad and comfortless. The little ones and myself are shut up in the wagons from the rain. Still it will find its way in and many things are wet; and take us all together we are a poor looking set, and all this for Oregon. I am thinking while I write, "Oh, Oregon, you must be a wonderful country." (Came 18 miles today.)

**The Knights made it to Oregon, arriving on September 13th. The slow and dangerous journey they made by wagon train now takes only a few hours by airplane. Given all the difficulties, why do you think so many people chose to make the westward journey on the Oregon Trail?**

Source: Amelia Stewart Knight, *Transactions of the Oregon Pioneer Association,* 1928.

# When I First Came to This Land

*From its beginnings to the present day, our nation has been shaped by the movement of people into and within the country. This song tells of some of the difficulties an immigrant faces in a new land. Why do you think the singer repeats that the land is "sweet and good"?*

Words and Music by Oscar Brand

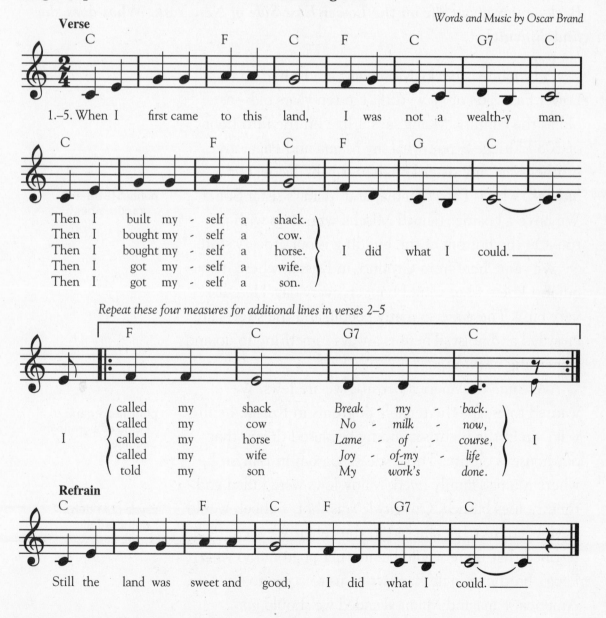

**Verse**

1.–5. When I first came to this land, I was not a wealth-y man.

Then I built my - self a shack.
Then I bought my - self a cow.
Then I bought my - self a horse. } I did what I could. _____
Then I got my - self a wife.
Then I got my - self a son.

*Repeat these four measures for additional lines in verses 2–5*

I { called my shack Break - my - back. } I
  called my cow No - milk - now,
  called my horse Lame - of - course,
  called my wife Joy - of-my - life
  told my son My work's done.

**Refrain**

Still the land was sweet and good, I did what I could. _____

Source: Oscar Brand. New York: Ludlow Music, Inc., 1957.

# Immigrant Girl

## by Brett Harvey

*In the early 1900s many immigrants from eastern Europe settled in New York City. In this selection from a fact-based story, Becky Moscowitz explains why her family left Russia and describes her new life in America. What does Becky enjoy about life on the Lower East Side of New York? What does she find difficult?*

My name is Becky Moscowitz, and I live on the Lower East Side of New York. I'm ten years old—as old as the century, Mama says. I live on the fifth floor of 108 Eldridge Street with my Mama and Papa, my brother Max, my sister Dinah, our baby Jacob, our **bubbeh**, who is Papa's mama, and Mama's sister Sonia. We have a boarder named Mischa who lives with us, too. On the bottom of the building is our grocery store.

*bubbeh* **(BUB-eh):** grandmother

We came here from Grodno, in Russia, where it was quiet. I knew what would happen every day. Here it is very busy. There are so many people and the streets are crowded and noisy. There is always something to do and something new to see.

We came to America because we are Jews. We wanted to escape the terrible **pogroms** in Russia. I still wake up in the night screaming because I dream that our house is on fire. There was a pogrom in Bialystok, where Mama's family lived. Many Jews were killed and their houses burned. Our *zayde* was shot. Bubbeh would have been, too, but she hid in the cellar. We were terrified that there would be another pogrom. So when Papa's brother, Uncle Ben, wrote us to come to America, Papa and Mama decided we should go.

**pogrom:** organized killing of a group of people

*zayde* **(ZAY-deh):** grandfather

We have three rooms in our flat. Dinah and I sleep in the **parlor** with Mama and Papa and the baby. Mischa and Max sleep in the bedroom. Sonia sleeps in the kitchen with Bubbeh. In the evening, it feels like there are twenty people living in the flat instead of nine. It's hard for me to do my homework in the kitchen because there's such a racket. Max and Dinah are fighting, Jacob is fussing, Papa's reading out loud, and Bubbeh is cleaning. Sometimes I sneak out and sit on the fire escape just to be by myself.

**parlor:** living room

In the morning I have a lot to do. Mama and Papa have already gone downstairs to open the store, and Sonia has left for work. First I have to get water from the faucet in the hall. I bring Bubbeh her glass of hot water with lemon. "These old bones can't move without it," she says. I help Dinah get dressed and give Jacob his bottle. Mischa always seems to be in the way while I'm getting breakfast for Dinah and me. We have bread and **herring** in the morning. After Max empties the ash bin and I sweep the kitchen, we take the baby to Mama and Papa in the store. Then we go to school.

**herring:** a saltwater fish

Our school is four blocks away on Rivington Street. It is called Public School 20, and it looks like a castle made of red bricks. It is so big that at first it made me feel as small as a mouse. My teacher, Miss Reilly, smells like roses and has a lace hanky tucked in her sleeve. Miss Reilly says we have to clean our teeth with brushes, and she looks for dirt under our fingernails. I am learning English fast because I don't want to be a "greenie." That's what they call you when you're new in America. I still have trouble mixing up v's and w's. Once some children in my class laughed at me because I said "adwenture." Miss Reilly corrected me. I wanted to crawl under my desk and stay there. My favorite part of school is art class because everyone likes the pictures

I draw. I don't have to talk and be afraid of saying something wrong.

After school I take care of Dinah and Jacob. I wrap the baby up, put him in his little cart, and go out on the block. My friends Rachel and Sadie are there too with their baby brothers and sisters. We play jacks and **potsies** and jump rope. The middle of the street belongs to the boys, but sometimes they let us play **ring-a-levio** or prisoner's base with them.

**potsies:** sidewalk game, similar to hopscotch
**ring-a-levio:** tag

Whenever I find a piece of chalk, I make pictures on the pavement. Everyone watches. When the delivery wagons drive over the drawings, my friends yell, "Hey! Get off Becky's pictures!"

My brother Max is a "newsie." Every afternoon he and his friends go uptown to sell newspapers. He gives most of the money he makes to Mama and Papa, but he keeps a little for himself. It makes me boil that I can't go uptown like Max and make my own money even though I'm older than he is. Some girls are newsies, like my friend Pearl. But Mama says she needs me at home.

On Sunday, if Max has any money left over, he takes me to the **nickelodeon**. We've seen *The Schoolboy's Revenge* and *The Queen of the Ranch* and *Baby Swallows a Nickel*. Max and I could stay all day in the dark, watching the pictures moving on the screen....

**nickelodeon:** movie theater

*Immigrants often have to get used to a new language, neighborhood, and way of living. They also keep many of their own customs. Which customs are new for Becky Moscowitz? Which are from her life in Russia?*

Source: Brett Harvey, *Immigrant Girl: Becky of Eldridge Street.* New York: Holiday House, 1987.

# Childtimes

**by Eloise Greenfield and Lessie Jones Little**

*In the book Childtimes three generations of one African American family—a grandmother, mother, and daughter—write about their childhoods. Some of their memories are of Parmele, North Carolina. Through these memories we learn about life in a southern town. "Towns build up around work," the grandmother says. What meaning did this have for Parmele over the years? How and why did Parmele change?*

## Pattie Frances Ridley Jones
Born in Bertie County, North Carolina,
December 15, 1884

Towns build up around work, you know. People go and live where they can find jobs. And that's how Parmele got started.

At first, it was just a junction, a place where two railroads crossed. Two Atlantic Coast Line railroads, one running between Rocky Mount and Plymouth, and one running between Kinston and Weldon. Didn't too many people live around there then, and those that did were pretty much spread out.

Well, around 1888, a **Yankee** named Mr. Parmele came down from New York and looked the place over, and he saw all those big trees and decided to start a lumber company. Everybody knew what that meant. There were going to be jobs! People came from everywhere to get work. Was right little at that time, too little to know what was going on, but everybody says it was something to see how fast that town grew. All those people moving in and houses going up. They named the town after the man who made the jobs, and they called it *Pomma-lee*.

**Yankee:** someone from a state in the North

91

The lumber company hired a whole lot of people. They hired workers to lay track for those little railroads they call tram roads that they were going to run back and forth between the town and the woods. They hired lumberjacks to chop the trees down and cut them up into logs, and load them on the tram cars. They hired men to build the mill and put the machinery in, and millworkers to run the machines that would cut the logs into different sizes and dry them and make them nice and smooth. . . .

Well, after a good many years—about eighteen, I guess—the mill had to be closed down. Just about all of those great big trees were gone. Mr. Parmele moved his lumber mill away, to South Carolina if I remember right, and that didn't leave too many jobs in our town. A lot of people left, a lot of people. They moved to other places, looking for work.

## Lessie Blanche Jones Little
### Born in Parmele, North Carolina,
### October 1, 1906

I used to hear Papa and Mama and their friends talking about the lumber mill that had been the center of life in Parmele before I was born, but there wasn't any mill when I was growing up. The only thing left of it was the sawdust from all the wood they had sawed there. The sawdust was about a foot thick on the land where the mill had been. I used to love to walk on it. It was spongy, and it made me feel like I was made of rubber. I'd take my shoes off and kind of bounce along on top of it. But that was all that was left of the mill.

My Parmele was a train town. The life of my town moved around the trains that came in and out all day long. About three hundred people lived in Parmele, most of them black. . . .

Most of the men and women in Parmele earned their living by farming. Some did other things like working at the tobacco factory in Robersonville, but most worked on the farms that were all around in the area, white people's farms usually. When I was a little girl, they earned fifty cents a day, a farm day, sunup to sundown, plus meals. After they got home, they had all their own work to do, cooking and cleaning, laundry, chopping wood for the woodstove, and shopping.

I used to love to go shopping with Mama. There was so much to see downtown. When people started getting cars, the only gasoline pump in town was down there. There were stores, four or five stores, where you could buy clothes, or yard goods, or groceries, or hardware, and the post office was in the corner of one store. . . .

Parmele had trains coming in and going out all day long. Passenger trains and **freight trains**. There was always so much going on at the station that I wouldn't know what to watch. People were changing trains and going in and out of the cafe and the restaurant. They came from big cities like New York and Chicago and Boston, and they were all wearing the latest styles. Things were being unloaded, like furniture and trunks and plows and cases of fruit and crates of clucking chickens, or a puppy. . . .

**freight trains:** trains that carry goods

The train station was a gathering place, too. A lot of people went there to relax after they had finished their work for the day. They'd come downtown to pick up their mail, or buy a newspaper, and then they'd just stand around laughing and talking to their friends. And on Sundays fellas and their girls would come all the way from other towns, just to spend the afternoon at the Parmele train station.

## Eloise Glynn Little Greenfield
Born in Parmele, North Carolina,
May 17, 1929

I grew up in Washington, D.C. Every summer we took a trip down home. Down home was Parmele.

To get ready for our trip, Daddy would spend days working on our old car, putting it in shape to go on the road, and Mama would wash and iron all of our clothes. Then everything would be packed in the tan leather suitcase and the black cardboard suitcase, and we'd be ready to go.

Mama and Daddy would sit in the front with Vedie in Mama's lap, and Wilbur, Gerald, and I sat in the back with our legs on top of the suitcases. This was before cars had trunks. Or radios. Or air conditioners or heaters. And there were no superhighways. The **speed limit** was forty-five miles an hour, and we went thirty-five to keep from straining the car.

**speed limit:** how fast or slow cars are allowed to go

It was an eight-hour trip to Norfolk, Virginia, where we always went first. Grandma Pattie Ridley Jones and Grandpa had moved there by that time, and we'd spend about a week with them, then go on to Parmele for another week. . . .

By the time of my visits there, only a few trains were still passing through. My Parmele wasn't a train town or a mill town. It was a quiet town. Chinaberry trees and pump water and tree swings and figs and fat, **pulpy** grapes on the vine. People saying "hey" instead of "hi," the way they did in Washington, *hey-ey*, sending their voices up, then down, softly, singing it through their noses. Parmele was me running from the chickens when I was little, riding around the yard in a goat-pulled cart, sitting on the porch and letting people going by in their cars wave at me, reading in the rocking chair, taking long walks to the gas station for soda pop with the children of Mama's and Daddy's childtime friends. Parmele was uncles and aunts and cousins. And Granny. And Pa.

**pulpy:** juicy

*What role did transportation play in Parmele? How did it change from one generation to the next?*

Source: Eloise Greenfield and Lessie Jones Little, *Childtimes*. New York: HarperCollins, 1979.

# Ancestry

**by Ashley Bryan**

*Our ancestors are the family members who came before us, like our grandparents and great-grandparents and great-great-grandparents. When we think of these people and their ways of life, we are remembering our ancestry. People in the United States have ancestors from many different countries. Where are ancestors of the child in this poem from?*

I splash in the ocean
My big brother watches me
We sing,
  "Wade in the water
  Wade in the water, children"

Mom and Dad
Teaching us **spirituals**
Reading us African tales
Singing songs
Telling stories
Reminding us
Of our ancestry

**spirituals:** religious folk songs or hymns

On the beach
Other children
Dig to China
I dig
To Africa

*Why do you think it is important to the parents of the child in this poem to remind their children of their ancestry? Why do you think people consider their ancestry to be an important part of who they are?*

Source: Ashley Bryan, *Sing to the Sun.* New York: HarperCollins, 1992.

# Halmoni and the Picnic

## by Sook Nyul Choi

*Feeling at home in a new culture can take some time. In this selection from a longer story, Yunmi's grandmother—Halmoni—is having trouble getting used to life in America, where she has been for only two months. Halmoni is afraid to speak English, and so she cannot talk to many of the people she meets. Yunmi's friends want to make Halmoni feel at home. They go to class wondering how to show Halmoni that they want to be her friends. What do they decide? What does Yunmi fear?*

"Children, I have a special announcement to make this morning," Mrs. Nolan said. "Next Tuesday is our **annual** picnic in **Central Park**. We need a **chaperon**, so please ask your parents if one of them can come and help us."

Helen and Anna Marie raised their arms high, nearly falling off their chairs. Surprised, Mrs. Nolan said, "Yes, Helen, you first. What is it?"

Helen blushed, then asked, "Can Yunmi's grandmother be our chaperon, please?"

**annual:** yearly
**Central Park:** a large park in New York City
**chaperon:** adult supervisor

Mrs. Nolan said, "Of course. But Yunmi must ask her grandmother first. Will you, Yunmi?"

Helen and Anna Marie grinned and nodded at Yunmi with excitement. But Yunmi was suddenly confused and worried. What if Halmoni did not want to come? What if the children made fun of her pointed rubber shoes and her long Korean dress?

That afternoon Yunmi cautiously told Halmoni what had happened at school.

Halmoni blushed with pleasure. "Helen said that? Your teacher wants me?"

So relieved to see Halmoni looking happy, Yunmi nodded her head up and down.

Touching Yunmi's cheek, Halmoni asked, "And do you want me to go to the picnic with you?"

"Yes, yes, Halmoni, it will be fun. You will meet all my friends, and Mrs. Nolan, and we will be together all day long in Central Park."

"Then yes, I will come," Halmoni said.

Halmoni would not go to the picnic empty-handed. She prepared a huge fruit basket for the third graders. She also insisted on making large plates of kimbap and a big jug of barley tea. Kimbap is made of rice, carrots, eggs, and green vegetables wrapped in seaweed. Again, Yunmi was worried. Most of the children would bring bologna or peanut butter sandwiches, which they would wash down with soda pop. What if no one wanted to eat Halmoni's kimbap? What if they made faces?

"Halmoni, please do not take the kimbap to the picnic. It took you so long to make. Let's save it for us to eat later."

"Oh, it was no problem. It looks so pretty and it's perfect for picnics. I wonder if I made enough."

On the morning of the picnic, Yunmi and her grandmother met the bus at school. Halmoni wore her pale blue skirt and top, called a ch'ima and chogori in Korean, with her white socks and white pointed rubber shoes.

When they arrived at Central Park, Halmoni sat under a big chestnut tree and watched the children play. The children took off their jackets and threw them in front of Halmoni. Smiling, she picked them up, shook off the grass and dirt, and folded each of them neatly. She liked the cool earth beneath her and the ringing laughter of the children.

At lunchtime, Halmoni placed the plates of kimbap on a large blue and white silk table cloth. Mrs. Nolan came over and gasped. "Oh, how beautiful they look! Children, come over and look at this. Yunmi's grandmother made my favorite lunch." Halmoni gave Mrs. Nolan a pair of chopsticks and poured a bit of soy sauce into a small dish. As the children munched on their sandwiches, they gathered around and watched Mrs. Nolan pop the little pieces of kimbap into her mouth.

Halmoni picked up one kimbap with her chopsticks and held it out to Helen. "Mogobwa," she said, which means "Try it." Helen understood and opened her mouth. Everyone watched her expression carefully as she chewed the strange-looking food. Her cautious chewing turned to delight. "Ummm, it's good!"

Then, Halmoni picked up another one and held it out for Anna Marie. "Nodo," she said, which means "You too." Anna Marie chewed slowly and then her face brightened, too. Helen and Anna Marie were ready for seconds, and soon everyone was eating the kimbap.

Halmoni smiled, displaying all her teeth. She forgot that in Korea it is not **dignified** for a woman to smile in public without covering her mouth with her hand.

**dignified:** proper

After lunch, some children asked Halmoni to hold one end of their jump rope. Others asked if Halmoni would make kimbap again for next year's picnic. When Yunmi translated, Halmoni nodded and said, "Kurae, kurae," meaning "Yes, yes."

The children started to chant as they jumped rope:
> "One, two, pointed shoe.
> Three, four, kimbap more.

Five, six, chopsticks.

Seven, eight, kimbap plate.

Kurae, kurae, Picnic Day!"

Halmoni smiled until tears clouded her vision. Her long blue ch'ima danced in the breeze as she turned the jump rope. She tapped her shoes to the rhythm of their song.

Mrs. Nolan asked Yunmi, "What should the class call your grandmother? Mrs. Lee?"

Yunmi said, "I just call her Halmoni, which means grandmother. In Korea, it is rude to call elders by their names."

Mrs. Nolan nodded and smiled. "Children, why don't we all thank Halmoni for her delicious kimbap?"

"Thank you for the kimbap, Halmoni!" the children shouted in unison. Halmoni's wrinkled face turned red and she looked down at her pointed shoes. She took a handkerchief from the large sleeve of her chogori and wiped her eyes.

Halmoni was deep in thought as the big bus wove through the New York City streets. When the bus arrived back at school, the children hurried off, shouting goodbye. Halmoni murmured in English, "Goodbye, goodbye."

Filled with pride, Yunmi grabbed Halmoni's hand and gave it a squeeze. Halmoni squeezed back. Yunmi grinned, thinking of Halmoni's big smile as the children sang about her in Central Park. Skipping along Fourteenth Street, Yunmi hummed the kimbap song.

She thought she heard Halmoni quietly humming along, too.

*The picnic gives the children a chance to welcome Halmoni into their community and to try something from Korea. What does it mean to Halmoni that the children eat and enjoy the kimbap she has prepared? Can you name some foods that other immigrant groups have brought to this country? Perhaps some of them—like hamburgers (from Germany), sandwiches (from England), egg rolls (from China), pizza (from Italy), or tacos (from Mexico)—are among your favorites!*

Source: Sook Nyul Choi, *Halmoni and the Picnic.* New York: Houghton Mifflin, 1993.

# IN A NEIGHBORHOOD IN LOS ANGELES

## by Francisco X. Alarcón

*Many Mexicans have come to live in the United States. The poet Francisco X. Alarcón is a Mexican American who was born in Los Angeles. In this poem he remembers his grandmother who took care of him when he was young. What did he learn from her?*

**En un Barrio de Los Angeles**
el español
lo aprendí
de mi abuela

mijito
no llores
me decía

en las mañanas
cuando salían
mis padres

a trabajar
en las canerías
de pescado

mi abuela
platicaba
con las sillas

les cantaba
canciones
antiguas

les bailaba
valses en
la cocina

cuando decía
niño barrigón
se reía

**In a Neighborhood in Los Angeles**
I learned
Spanish
from my grandma

**mijito**
don't cry
she'd tell me

on the mornings
my parents
would leave

to work
at the fish
**canneries**

my grandma
would chat
with chairs

sing them
old
songs

dance
waltzes with them
in the kitchen

when she'd say
**niño barrigón**
she'd laugh

**mijito:** my grandson

**canneries:** factories where food is put into cans

**niño barrigón:** chubby little boy

100

con mi abuela
aprendí
a contar nubes

with my grandma
I learned
to count clouds

a reconocer
en las macetas
la yerbabuena

to point out
in flowerpots
mint leaves

mi abuela
llevaba lunas
en el vestido

my grandma
wore moons
on her dress

la montaña
el desierto
el mar de México

Mexico's mountains
deserts
ocean

en sus ojos
yo los veía
en sus trenzas

in her eyes
I'd see them
in her braids

yo los tocaba
con su voz
yo los olia

I'd touch them
in her voice
smell them

un día
me dijeron
se fue muy lejos

one day
I was told:
she went far away

pero yo aún
las siento
conmigo

but still
I feel her
with me

diciéndome
quedito al oído
mijito

whispering
in my ear
*mijito*

*The poet's grandmother taught him things about Mexican culture. She taught him Spanish and old songs and dances, and she reminded him of Mexico. What have you learned about your culture from people you know?*

Source: Francisco X. Alarcón, *Body in Flames/Cuerpo en Llamas*. San Francisco, CA: Chronicle Books, 1990.

# Success!

## telegram sent by Orville Wright

*On December 17, 1903, Orville Wright made the world's first successful airplane flight while his brother, Wilbur, ran alongside the plane that the two had invented. How did the Wright brothers announce the news? By telegram. Read Orville's message outloud. Where do you pause between thoughts?*

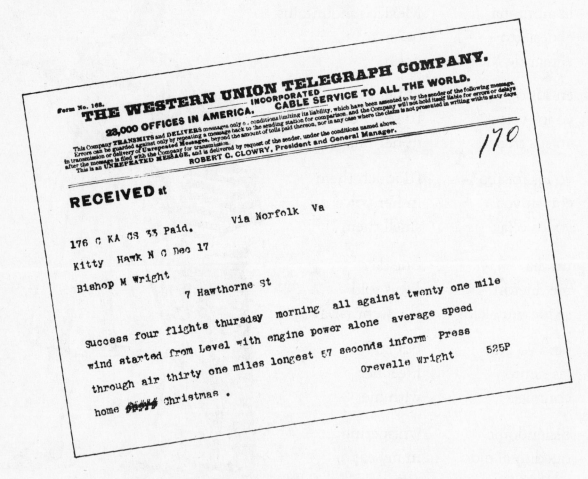

*In sending the telegram from one place to another, two changes were made to the message. The first was that the longest flight of the day was written as 57 seconds when it should have been 59. The second was that Orville's name was misspelled! What technology would you tell Orville to use if he were sending his message today? Why?*

Source: Russell Freedman, *The Wright Brothers: How They Invented the Airplane.* New York: Holiday House, 1991.

# Amelia Takes To The Skies

## by Navidad O'Neill

*Amelia Earhart (1897–1937) was a famous airplane pilot in the 1920s and 1930s. She was the first woman to fly over the Atlantic Ocean alone and the first person to fly over it twice. She was also the first woman to make a round-trip flight across the United States. Since there weren't many airports in those days, Earhart sometimes had to land in strange places. In the town of Pecos, Texas, she once landed right in the middle of Main Street! Why do you think Earhart is a hero to the children in this play?*

### CAST OF CHARACTERS

**Amelia Earhart,** *pilot*

**Betty**
**Billy**
**Sidney**    *children from Pecos, Texas*
**Camille**
**Jackson**
**Tiffany**

**Time:** *1928*
**Place:** *Pecos, Texas*

*Six friends bend their necks to stare up at the sky.*

**Betty:** Hear anything?

**Billy:** Nope.

**Sidney:** See anything?

**Camille:** Not yet.

**Jackson:** Think she's up there?

**Tiffany:** They say she is.

**Betty:** A woman flying through the sky!

**Billy:** It's hard to believe.

**Sidney:** You sure it's true?

**Camille:** She crossed the Atlantic Ocean, didn't she?

**Jackson:** But she wasn't the pilot then. Now she's all alone in her plane.

**Betty:** A woman flying through the sky!

**Tiffany:** Amelia, are you up there?

**Billy:** Amelia Earhart, you're our hero!

**Betty:** Someday I'll be a pilot like you.

**Camille:** She's so brave!

**Jackson:** Hear anything?

**Tiffany:** My grandfather said people will go back to horses soon.

**Betty:** My grandfather said soon everyone will have cars, and someday people will fly in airships.

**Billy:** Wait, listen.

**Sidney:** Do you hear that soft rumble?

**Camille:** I hear a faraway roar.

**Jackson:** Maybe it's her.

**Tiffany:** It can't be.

**Betty:** Can't be? Look up there!

**Billy:** It's a bird.

**Sidney:** No it's not.

**Camille:** It's Amelia Earhart.

**Jackson:** But this is Main Street!

**Tiffany:** There's no runway here.

**Sidney:** Clear the street! She's coming in for a landing!

*All the children run to the sides of the stage. Enter Amelia Earhart. The children all cheer and run to greet her.*

**Amelia:** I understand this is Pecos, Texas, is that right?

**All:** Yes! Why are you here in our town?

**Amelia:** Well, you heard I was flying across the country didn't you?

**All:** Yes!

**Amelia:** When I saw this nice Main Street, I thought this was a good place to land. I need to work on one of my engine valves.

**All:** Amelia Earhart landed in our town!

**Amelia:** If you can point me to a garage, I think I'll borrow some tools. It seems I have a lot of work to do on my engine.

**Camille:** Do you know how to fix an airplane engine?

**Amelia:** Sure do. I know just about everything I can know about how my plane works. I can take apart the engine, and I can sew up the canvas sides if they rip.

**Billy:** You can fly a plane and fix its engine!

**Amelia:** Sure, just like my car. If I'm going to drive it, I want to know how it works.

**Tiffany:** You mean you have your own car?!

**Betty:** And you can work on your car's engine, too?

**Amelia:** Sure. I love knowing how things work.

**Jackson:** Is that why you're flying across country?

**Amelia:** I want to show that flying isn't just for men. I want to show that women can be free to live their lives just as men are. Now, if you'll excuse me, I have a lot of work to do before I can take off to the skies again.

*She exits. All the children wave goodbye.*

**Sidney:** After that day, we all followed Amelia Earhart's adventures in the newspaper.

**Betty:** Since she wasn't the pilot the first time she crossed the Atlantic, she wanted to do it again by herself.

**Billy:** And she did. On May 20, 1932, she left Newfoundland, Canada, exactly five years after Charles Lindbergh became the first man to fly alone across the Atlantic.

**Tiffany:** She carried two cans of tomato juice, a comb, a toothbrush, and a twenty-dollar bill.

**Jackson:** It was a rough trip. She hit a storm. Ice formed on the wings of the plane and Amelia's plane spun and almost hit the ocean.

**Sidney:** But she made it to Ireland, and when she came home the National Geographic Society honored her as the first woman to fly over the Atlantic, the first woman to fly over it alone, and the first PERSON in the world to cross it twice.

*The children all look up.*

**Betty:** A woman flying through the sky!

**All:** We'll never forget you, Amelia!

## THE END

*Amelia Earhart went on to make other daring flights, including one from Hawaii to California, this time over the Pacific Ocean. A few days before her 40th birthday, Earhart disappeared. She was three days away from completing a flight around the world. No one knows what happened to her. Her plane was never found. What questions would you ask Amelia Earhart if you could speak to her today?*

# The First Ride
## *Blazing the Trail for the Pony Express*

### by Jacqueline Geis

*The Pony Express was a mail service started in 1860 to deliver mail across the western United States by horseback. Mail was handed-off from one brave rider to the next. You can see the map of the route the riders followed on page 251 of your textbook. This fact-based story is told in the voice of a Pony Express rider. What dangers did the riders face?*

In 1860, I was hired by the Central Overland California and Pike's Peak Express Company to ride for the Pony Express. I was given a small Bible and was asked to sign a pledge. All riders had to promise never to use bad language, drink alcohol, or fight with other riders. We also had to promise to be honest and faithful in our jobs and to use our weapons only in self-defense.

Riders traveled both ways—east and west—on the Pony Express trail. The ride west started in St. Joseph,

Missouri, while the ride east began in Sacramento, California. I was the first eastbound rider, picking up mail in Sacramento and carrying it to my home station at Sportsman's Hall. There I would wait for a little over nine days for the westbound mail to reach me. Then it would be back to Sacramento, carrying news of the east to that city.

Our orders were to stay on schedule, no matter what happened.

Our motto was: "The mail must go through."

As the sun was peeking through the snow clouds, my first eastbound ride was coming to an end. I could see my home station up ahead in the town of Sportsman's Hall. It was a welcome sight, for I had just ridden sixty miles east from Sacramento, and I was tired and cold.

The stationkeeper grabbed my sturdy, snorting mustang as I arrived. He gave my leather mail pouch— called a *mochila* (moe-CHEE-la)—to the waiting rider and sent him on his way toward the east.

"What's your name, son?" asked the stationkeeper.

"Billy Hamilton," I replied through my chattering teeth. Wiping my red, runny nose on my sleeve, I went inside the cabin to warm myself. As I stood in front of the fire, the feeling in my numb-to-the-bones fingers returned. My stomach began to howl like a coyote as the smell of bacon and beans in a pot hanging over the flames tickled and tempted my nose.

After I had hung my cold, wet clothes by the fire, the stationkeeper came in. He stomped the snow from his boots and rustled up a plate of beans and cornbread and a tin cup of coffee for me. For the next nine days we would share chores, dreams, and tall tales of the trail, waiting while other Pony Express riders carried the westbound mail toward my station.

Just fifteen hours before I arrived at Sportsman's Hall, a celebration had begun in the town of St. Joseph,

Missouri. Flags of all kinds and colors rippled and waved from the town buildings while a brass band played. Men, women, and children, dressed in their best, had come to see the westbound Pony Express take off for the two-thousand-mile trip to Sacramento, California.

The thought that mail could reach the west coast in only ten days was almost impossible to believe. In the excitement, the crowd spooked the horse chosen for the first run. Some even tried to pull hairs from her tail to keep as souvenirs.

The people in the crowd became restless when they were told that the train carrying the mail from Washington, D.C., was more that two hours late. At last they heard the whistle of the train and the sound of the engine rushing and roaring at the edge of town.

A cannon fired a smoky salute after the mayor and company officials shouted their speeches. Johnny Fry was dressed in a red shirt, blue jeans, boots, and slouch hat, and carried a shiny revolver in a "Slim Jim" holster. He put the mochila on his saddle and mounted his horse. He rode a few blocks to the west, to the ferryboat that would float him across the Missouri River to Elwood in Kansas Territory.

After the ferry docked, Fry continued on his way, racing toward the west. He had started two-and-a-half hours behind schedule, so he rode hard from relay station to station in order to make up the lost time.

Don Rising, who was barely old enough to grow a beard, took the mochila from Johnny Fry at Seneca and carried it to Marysville. The leather mochila was used to carry the mail because it fit over the saddle and was easily passed from one rider to the next. Attached to the mochila were four boxes called *cantinas* (kan-TEE-nuz). Three cantinas were locked and one was kept open to receive the mail. The locked cantinas could only be opened with keys guarded in the post offices at St. Joseph and Sacramento.

Rising arrived in Marysville just about the time I was settling in at Sportsman's Hall.

Jack Keetley, waiting at the Marysville station, grabbed the mochila from Rising and carried it through the stations called Hollenburg, Rock Creek, and Big Sandy.

Henry Wallace, on his Kentucky-bred horse, rode through the prairie grass so fast he could set it on fire. He took the mochila through Liberty Farm and on to Fort Kearny.

Immigrants who were riding in a stagecoach on the Oregon Trail strained their necks, like turtles in their shells, to get a glimpse of a Pony Express rider passing by. The rider was Barney Wintle, headed for Cottonwood Springs, hunched down in the saddle behind his horse's mane....

Some think the eastbound and westbound riders passed each other somewhere east of Salt Lake City. An eagle in the sky was probably the only witness to this event.

Richard Egan galloped across the wide desert floor, blinking his eyes at the mirages he saw on his seventy-five-mile trip to Rush Valley.

William Dennis took over next, blazing a trail to Egan Canyon.

William Fisher rode through mountain ranges where every rock, tree, and trail looked the same as ten others, making it easy to get lost. A skillful explorer, Fisher found his home station at Ruby Valley.

With every change in the wind, "Pony Bob" Haslam breathed in scents of sagebrush and juniper on his route from Buckland's Station, past Carson City, and west to Friday's Station.

While I waited, Warren Upson was riding through the Sierra Nevada Mountains toward my home station. His horse picked his way carefully through the dangerous, narrow trail between the granite cliffs. Upson, in awe of the towering heights, looked toward the sky at clouds that appeared to beckon to him and guide him safely through the stony passages to Sportsman's Hall.

I heard the rumbling of hoofbeats in the distance and turned in time to see Upson's hat fly off his head. My wait was over. Upson threw me the mochila, and I was on my way.

I was off on my ride back to Sacramento. Remembering my company pledge, I couldn't have been stopped by a blizzard, an earthquake, or a shower of arrows.

Judging the time by watching the sun sink lower in the sky, I knew I was getting close to Sacramento. By dusk, I had reached the edge of town, riding behind a cloud of dust from lookout messengers who rode ahead of me. A bonfire in the street lit the cheering faces of the townspeople. At last their isolation from the rest of the country was ended.

*Eighteen months after the first ride of the Pony Express, telegraph lines reached California, and mail delivery by horse went out of business. But while it lasted, the young men who rode from St. Joseph, Missouri, to Sacramento, California, made the Pony Express a legend. What skills and special traits do you suppose a Pony Express rider needed?*

Source: Jacqueline Geis, *The First Ride: Blazing the Trail for the Pony Express.* Nashville: Hambleton-Hill, 1995.

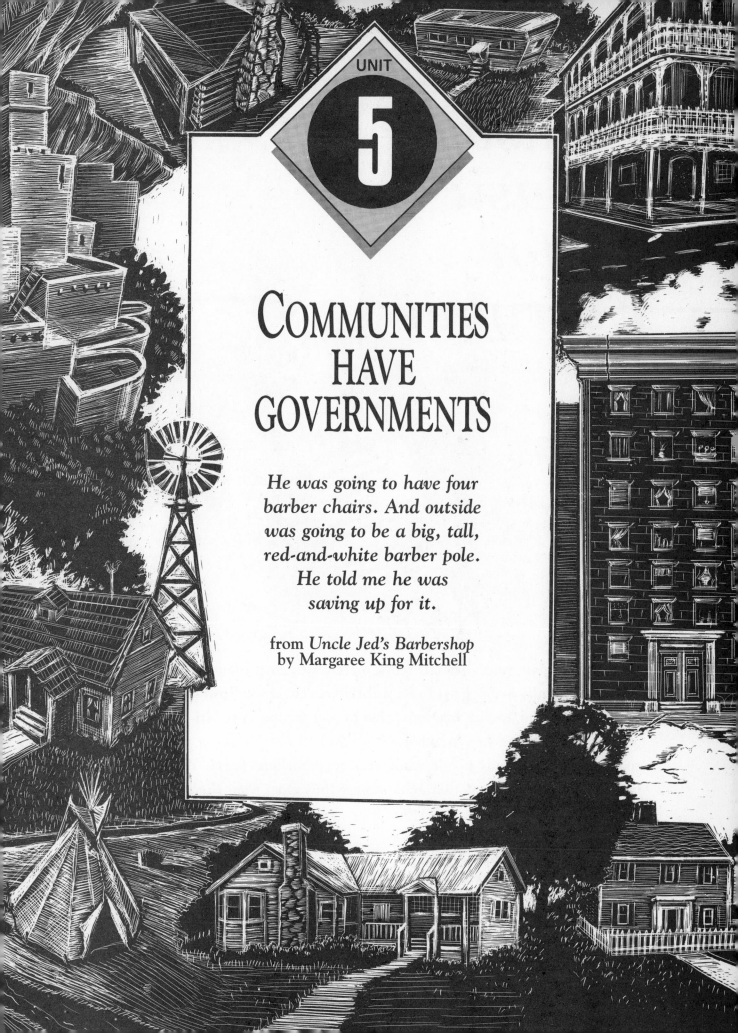

# COMMUNITIES HAVE GOVERNMENTS

*He was going to have four
barber chairs. And outside
was going to be a big, tall,
red-and-white barber pole.
He told me he was
saving up for it.*

from *Uncle Jed's Barbershop*
by Margaree King Mitchell

# Music, Music for Everyone

by Vera B. Williams

*In this story four young friends work together to earn money. The money jar Rosa's family keeps used to be full. However, since Rosa's grandmother became sick, the jar has been emptied to pay for her care. In order to fill the jar again, Rosa and her friends form a band. It takes a lot of practice, but soon the band is ready to entertain at a neighborhood party. What do the band members plan to do with the money they earn from their first job?*

*O*ur big chair often sits in our living room empty now. When I first got my accordion, Grandma and Mama used to sit in that chair together to listen to me practice. And every day after school while Mama was at her job at the diner, Grandma would be sitting in the chair by the window. Even if it was snowing big flakes down on her hair, she would lean way out to call, "Hurry up, Pussycat. I've got something nice for you."

But now Grandma is sick. She has to stay upstairs in the big bed in Aunt Ida and Uncle Sandy's extra room. Mama and Aunt Ida and Uncle Sandy and I take turns taking care of her. When I come home from school, I run right upstairs to ask Grandma if she wants anything. I carry up the soup Mama has left for her. I water her plants and report if the **Christmas cactu**s has any flowers yet. Then I sit on her bed and tell her about everything.

**Christmas cactus:** a cactus that blooms every winter

Grandma likes it when my friends Leora, Jenny, and Mae come home with me because we play music for her. Leora plays the drums. Mae plays the flute. Jenny plays fiddle and I play my accordion. One time we played a dance for Grandma that we learned in the music club at school.

Grandma clapped until it made her too tired. She told us it was like the music in the village where she lived when she was a girl. It made her want to dance right down the street. We had to keep her from trying to hop out of bed to go to the kitchen to fix us a treat.

Leora and Jenny and Mae and I left Grandma to rest and went down to get our own treat. We squeezed together into our big chair to eat it.

"It feels sad down here without your grandma," Leora said. "Even your big money jar up there looks sad and empty."

"Remember how it was full to the top and I couldn't even lift it when we bought the chair for my mother?" I said.

"And remember how it was more than half full when you got your accordion?" Jenny said.

"I bet it's empty now because your mother has to spend all her money to take care of your grandma till she gets better. That's how it was when my father had his accident and couldn't go to work for a long time," Mae said.

Mae had a dime in her pocket and she dropped it into the jar. "That will make it look a little fuller anyway," she said as she went home.

But after Jenny and Leora and Mae went home, our jar looked even emptier to me. I wondered how we would ever be able to fill it up again while Grandma was sick. I wondered when Grandma would be able to come downstairs again. Even our beautiful chair with roses all over it seemed empty with just me in the corner of it. The whole house seemed so empty and so quiet.

I got out my accordion and I started to play. The notes sounded beautiful in the empty room. One song that is an old tune sounded so pretty I played it over and over. I remembered what my mother had told me about my other grandma and how she used to play the accordion. Even when she was a girl not much bigger than I, she would get up and play at a party or a wedding so the company could dance and sing. Then people would stamp their feet and yell, "More, more!" When they went home, they would leave money on the table for her.

That's how I got my idea for how I could help fill up the jar again. I ran right upstairs. "Grandma," I whispered. "Grandma?"

"Is that you, Pussycat?" she answered in a sleepy voice. "I was just having such a nice dream about you. Then I woke up and heard you playing that beautiful old song. Come. Sit here and brush my hair."

I brushed Grandma's hair and told her my whole idea. She thought it was a great idea. "But tell the truth, Grandma," I begged her. "Do you think kids could really do that?"

"I think you and Jenny and Leora and Mae could do it. No question. No question at all," she answered.

"Only don't wait a minute to talk to them about it. Go call and ask them now."

And that was how the Oak Street Band got started.

Our music teachers helped us pick out pieces we could all play together. Aunt Ida, who plays guitar, helped us practice. We practiced on our back porch. One day our neighbor leaned out his window in his pajamas and yelled, "Listen, kids, you sound great but give me a break. I work at night. I've got to get some sleep in the daytime." After that we practiced inside. Grandma said it was helping her get better faster than anything.

At last my accordion teacher said we sounded very good. Uncle Sandy said so too. Aunt Ida and Grandma said we were terrific. Mama said she thought anyone would be glad to have us play for them.

It was Leora's mother who gave us our first job. She asked us to come and play at a party for Leora's great-grandmother and great-grandfather. It was going to be a special **anniversary** for them. It was fifty years ago on that day they first opened their market on our corner. Now Leora's mother takes care of the market. She always plays the radio loud while she works. But for the party she said there just had to be live music.

**anniversary:** yearly celebration

All of Leora's aunts and uncles and cousins came to the party. Lots of people from our block came too. Mama and Aunt Ida and Uncle Sandy walked down from our house very slowly with Grandma. It was Grandma's first big day out.

There was a long table in the backyard made from little tables all pushed together. It was covered with so many big dishes of food you could hardly see the tablecloth. But I was too excited to eat anything.

Leora and Jenny and Mae and I waited over by the rosebush. Each of us had her instrument all ready. But everyone else went on eating and talking and eating some more. We didn't see how they would ever get around to listening to us. And we didn't see how we could be brave enough to begin.

At last Leora's mother pulled us right up in front of everybody. She banged on a pitcher with a spoon to get attention.

Then she introduced each one of us. "And *now* we're going to have music," she said. "Music and dancing for everyone."

It was quiet as school assembly. Every single person there was looking right at Leora and Jenny and Mae and me. But we just stood there and stared right back.

Then I heard my grandma whisper, "Play Pussycat. Play anything. Just like you used to play for me."

I put my fingers on the keys and buttons of my accordion. Jenny tucked her fiddle under her chin. Mae put her flute to her mouth. Leora held up her drums. After that we played and played. We made mistakes, but we played like a real band. The little lanterns came on. Everyone danced.

Mama and Aunt Ida and Uncle Sandy smiled at us every time they danced by. Grandma kept time nodding her head and tapping with the cane she uses now. Leora and Jenny and Mae and I forgot about being scared. We loved the sound of the Oak Street Band.

And afterward everybody clapped and shouted. Leora's great-grandfather and great-grandmother thanked us. They said we had made their party something they would always remember. Leora's father piled up plates of food for us. My mamma arranged for Leora, Jenny, and Mae to stay over at our house. And when we finally all went out the gate together, late at night, Leora's mother tucked an envelope with our money into Leora's pocket.

As soon as we got home, we piled into my bed to divide the money. We made four equal shares. Leora said she was going to save up for a bigger drum. Mae wasn't sure what she would do with her share. Jenny fell asleep before she could tell us. But I couldn't even lie down until I climbed up and put mine right into our big jar on the shelf near our chair.

*Vera Williams painted the pictures that go with this story. To see more of her artwork, check the book out from your library.*

Source: Vera B. Williams, *Music, Music for Everyone.* New York: Greenwillow, 1984.

# On the Job

## Selections from Interviews by Linda Scher

*Everywhere you look there are people at work. In school, at the store, at home—even on television, you can see people doing their jobs. How do people choose which jobs to do? How do they spend their time on the job? One way to find out is to talk to people about their work. In these interviews people with very different jobs talk about what they do. You have already met two of these people on the Infographic in your textbook on pages 284–285. What questions would you like to ask about their jobs?*

I work at the Big Bear grocery store. I do all the ordering of fruits and vegetables for the store. I write an order once a week based on our past records of how much we ordered the year before, so if you keep good records you can write a good order. All the fruits and vegetables we put out have to be gone through constantly so that we can remove the ones that are no longer fresh.

**Produce** is exciting because it's not the same job day in and day out. It's a seasonal job. This means that what we sell in the fruit and vegetable department depends on the time of year.

**produce:** fruits and vegetables

The most enjoyable part of the job for me is meeting people. I know hundreds of people that I would not have known working in an office. One of the hardest parts of the job is trying to satisfy everybody. Sometimes you just don't have what they want.

Brian Massie
*Grocery Store Produce Manager*
*Huntington, West Virginia*

I am a small-animal veterinarian. That means I take care of dogs, cats, and pocket pets like gerbils, hamsters, rats, guinea pigs, rabbits, parrots, and even wild birds. Most of my job is centered around teaching people how to take care of pets. I talk to pet owners about how to feed and care for their pets. I especially like working with the children to teach them how to take care of their pets, because the children are usually the ones that know their pets best. I like to heal animals. It makes me feel good when I can get them well. The most challenging part of my job is working with people to make them understand the needs of their pets.

Denice Burnham
*Veterinarian*
Orofino, Idaho

If you want to be a television reporter, the best training is to be interested in what is happening. Don't be afraid to learn things. You have to like history. You have to be aware of what is going on in other parts of the world.

The most difficult part of the job is really never knowing what you're going to do next. But it's also the most interesting. You never get bored doing this job. When new stories break, I have to be ready to find a way to make them understandable to the people who are watching television. Sometimes stories happen so fast that we don't have time for the writers to write anything for us to read to the television audience. I have to think about what I'm going to say as I'm saying it. It's great when it happens on something I'm prepared for. But it's scary when you have to talk on the air about something you know nothing about. Then you just have to be a regular person. I ask myself, "Well what would I want to find out?" When I talk to people on the air, I ask them the things that I would like to know.

Leon Harris
*Television Anchorperson*
Stone Mountain, Georgia

*You can read about another job in* Working on an Assembly Line, *pages 129–130. What job would you like to learn more about?*

# UNCLE JED'S
# *Barbershop*

## by Margeree King Mitchell

*In this story Sarah Jean's uncle Jed works and saves throughout his life to achieve his dream of opening a barbershop. As an African American in the early 1900s, Uncle Jed faces many challenges. Still he never gives up his goal. Over the years what events keep Uncle Jed from opening his own shop? How is he finally able to make his dream come true?*

Jedediah Johnson was my granddaddy's brother. Everybody has their favorite relative. Well, Uncle Jedediah was mine.

He used to come by our house every Wednesday night with his clippers. He was the only black barber in the county. Daddy said that before Uncle Jed started cutting hair, he and Granddaddy used to have to go thirty miles to get a haircut.

After Uncle Jed cut my daddy's hair, he lathered a short brush with soap and spread it over my daddy's face and shaved him. Then he started over on my granddaddy.

I always asked Uncle Jed to cut my hair, but Mama wouldn't let him. So he would run the clippers on the back of my neck and just pretend to cut my hair. He even spread lotion on my neck. I would smell wonderful all day.

When he was done, he would pick me up and sit me in his lap and tell me about the barbershop he was going to open one day and about all the fancy equipment that would be in it. The sinks would be so shiny they sparkled, the floors so clean you could see yourself. He was going to have four barber chairs. And outside was going to be a big, tall, red-and-white barber pole. He told me he was saving up for it.

He had been saying the same things for years. Nobody believed him. People didn't have dreams like that in those days.

We lived in the South. Most people were poor. My daddy owned a few acres of land and so did a few others. But most people were sharecroppers. That meant they lived in a shack and worked somebody else's land in exchange for a share of the crop.

When I was five years old, I got sick. This particular morning, I didn't come into the kitchen while Mama was fixing breakfast. Mama and Daddy couldn't wake me up. My nightgown and the bedclothes were all wet where I had sweated.

Mama wrapped me in a blanket while Daddy went outside and hitched the horse to the wagon. We had to travel about twenty miles into town to the hospital. It was midday when we got there. We had to go to the colored waiting room. In those days, they kept blacks and whites separate. There were separate public restrooms, separate water fountains, separate schools. It was called segregation. So in the hospital, we had to go to the colored waiting room.

Even though I was unconscious, the doctors wouldn't look at me until they had finished with all the white patients. When the doctors did examine me, they told my daddy that I needed an operation and that it would cost three hundred dollars.

Three hundred dollars was a lot of money in those days. My daddy didn't have that kind of money. And the doctors wouldn't do the operation until they had the money.

My mama bundled me back up in the blanket and they took me home. Mama held me in her arms all night. She kept me alive until Daddy found Uncle Jed. He found him early the next morning in the next county on his way to cut somebody's hair. Daddy told him about me.

Uncle Jed leaned on his bent cane and stared straight ahead. He told Daddy that the money didn't matter. He couldn't let anything happen to his Sarah Jean.

Well, I had the operation. For a long time after that, Uncle Jed came by the house every day to see how I was doing. I know that three hundred dollars delayed him from opening the barbershop.

Uncle Jed came awfully close to opening his shop a few years after my operation. He had saved enough money to buy the land and build the building. But he still needed money for the equipment.

Anyway, Uncle Jed had come by the house. We had just finished supper when there was a knock on the door. It was Mr. Ernest Walters, a friend of Uncle Jed's. He had come by to tell Uncle Jed about the bank failing. That was where Mr. Walters and Uncle Jed had their money. Uncle Jed had over three thousand dollars in the bank, and it was gone.

Uncle Jed just stood there a long time before he said anything. Then he told Mr. Walters that even though he was disappointed, he would just have to start all over again.

Talk about some hard times. That was the beginning of the Great Depression. Nobody had much money.

But Uncle Jed kept going around to his customers cutting their hair, even though they couldn't pay him. His customers shared with him whatever they had—a hot meal, fresh eggs, vegetables from the garden. And when they were able to pay again, they did.

And Uncle Jed started saving all over again.

Ol' Uncle Jed finally got his barbershop. He opened it on his seventy-ninth birthday. It had everything just like he said it would—big comfortable chairs, four cutting stations. You name it! The floors were so clean, they sparkled.

On opening day, people came from all over the county. They were Ol' Uncle Jed's customers. He had walked to see them for so many years. That day they all came to him.

I believe he cut hair all night and all the next day and the next night and the day after that! That man was so glad to have that shop, he didn't need any sleep.

Of course, I was there, too. I wouldn't have missed it for the world. When I sat in one of the big barber chairs, Uncle Jed patted the back of my neck with lotion like he always did. Then he twirled me round and round in the barber chair.

Uncle Jed died not long after that, and I think he died a happy man. You see, he made his dream come true even when nobody else believed in it.

He taught me to dream too.

*Do you already have a dream about the kind of work you would like to do? How do you think you can make your dream come true?*

Source: Margaree King Mitchell, *Uncle Jed's Barbershop*. New York: Simon & Schuster, 1993.

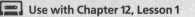

# The Cow

## by Robert Louis Stevenson

*This is a well-known poem about a familiar farm animal: the milk cow. Technology may have changed many things about farming, but it has not replaced "the friendly cow" who gives us milk and cream. What are some foods that can be made from milk?*

The friendly cow all red and white,
    I love with all my heart:
She gives me cream with all her might,
    To eat with apple-tart.

She wanders **lowing** here and there,        **lowing:** mooing
    And yet she cannot stray,
All in the pleasant open air,
    The pleasant light of day;

And blown by all the winds that pass
    And wet with all the showers,
She walks among the meadow grass
    And eats the meadow flowers.

*Which words would you use to describe the cow in this poem? How would you describe the farm where the cow grazes? Do there seem to be a lot of people in the scene? On the next page you can read a poem about a different kind of farm work.*

# Picking Berries

## by Aileen Fisher

*Many different kinds of berries are grown on fruit farms, and some grow wild in rural areas. Picking berries by hand can be lots of fun. But picking berries day after day, as some farm workers do, is very hard work. In the poem below, Aileen Fisher describes a day spent picking berries. What words does she repeat in the poem? Why do you think she does this?*

All day long
we picked and picked.

The sun was strong,
the bushes pricked.

The berries grew
in **brambly** places
where twigs untied
my sneaker laces.

**brambly:** full of thorns

We picked and picked
and picked some more.
The sun blazed down,
my arms got sore,

And then all night
as time went ticking
I dreamed I still
kept picking, picking.

*Compare this poem to "The Cow" on page 126. What differences do you notice? Which poem would you describe as "faster"? Why?*

Source: Lee Bennett Hopkins, ed., *On the Farm*. Boston: Little, Brown, 1991.

127

# Down in a Coal Mine
## Folk Song

*This song comes from the Monongahela Valley in Pennsylvania. It has been sung by coal miners for many years. What do you think it would be like to work "underneath the ground"?*

Down in the coal mine,

un - der - neath the ground,

Where a gleam of sun - shine

nev - er can be found;

Dig - ging dusk - y dia - monds

all the sea - son round,

Down in a coal mine,

un - der - neath the ground.

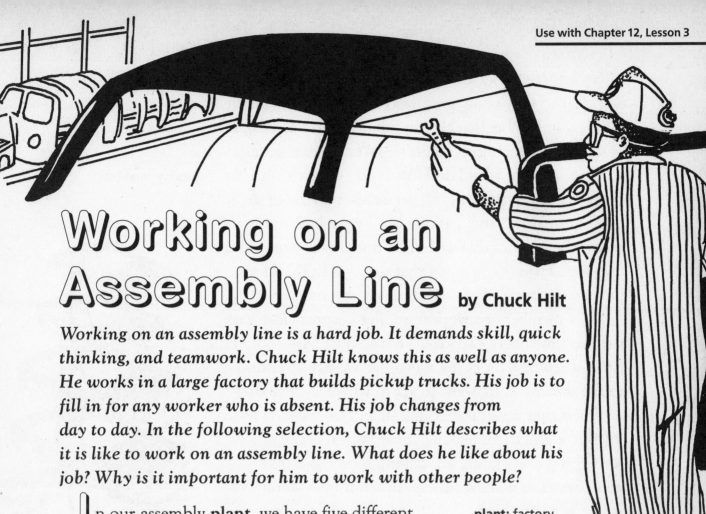

# Working on an Assembly Line

**by Chuck Hilt**

*Working on an assembly line is a hard job. It demands skill, quick thinking, and teamwork. Chuck Hilt knows this as well as anyone. He works in a large factory that builds pickup trucks. His job is to fill in for any worker who is absent. His job changes from day to day. In the following selection, Chuck Hilt describes what it is like to work on an assembly line. What does he like about his job? Why is it important for him to work with other people?*

In our assembly **plant**, we have five different departments: trim, cab shop, paint, **chassis**, and the final line. Each one of those departments **assembles** a part of the truck. All parts join at the final line to create a truck. And that's basically what our plant does: we assemble parts that are shipped to us. Some things come in **preassembled**, like seats. They're assembled at other places and we get them in **through freight**. Then we bolt them down and create a truck.

We have about 2,500 people working out here. I usually work in the trim area. My team handles all of the glass: the mirrors, the crank-up windows in the doors, and the windshields. We **install** all the parts related to glass, such as the door handles and the inside molding. When the body leaves trim, it goes over and meets up with the chassis department. This department assembles the engine, the wheels, and the frame. Then they drop the body down on the chassis. On the final line they put the front panels around the engine.

**plant:** factory

**chassis [chas´ĕ]:** frame that supports the body of a car

**asembles:** puts together

**preassembled:** already built

**through freight:** by transportation from other factories

**install:** put in place

Some people like knowing what they're going to be doing when they come in to work. They like to know they're going to be on a certain job. But I like coming in and doing different jobs. To me it makes the time go faster.

I take pride in what I do. I like to do a **quality** job. I like to try to do everything right. I get satisfaction out of seeing one of our trucks in a parking lot. I get a kick out of seeing the product that we built. I find myself wondering what job I was doing when that one was built, if I was putting in door pads or windshields or whatever.

quality: first-rate

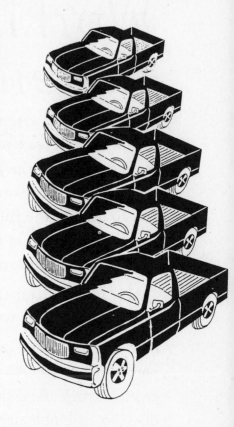

As a member of a work team, I've become close with the team members. We joke. That's how I pass a lot of time—keeping a lot of joking going. We pay attention to the job. We don't want to get to where we're joking so much that we let something slide. But cracking a joke now and then, making conversation about something that's going on, talking sports—all that contributes to making time go faster. If I get along well with my team, things seem to go a whole lot better.

This work is basically the same as a sports team. Same idea. Like a football team: you've got a quarterback, linemen, and running backs. When everybody does what they're supposed to do, then the play is successful. That's the same way with building a truck. One person can't build a truck. It takes a whole team. If one person lacks, or **slacks**, or isn't doing his job, or is not able to get something on, I might not be able to put my part on. And me not putting my part on might affect somebody else. That's why it's important for everybody to work together and make sure they do it right the first time.

slacks: slows

*Assembly-line workers like Chuck Hilt play a key role in our country's economy. They build products that people want and need. By providing jobs, factories make communities stronger. People like Chuck Hilt make these factories work to keep our country moving.*

Source: Adapted from Neil Johnson, *All in a Day's Work: Twelve Americans Talk About Their Jobs*. Boston: Little, Brown, and Company, 1989.

# No Star Nights

## by Anna Egan Smucker

*In the 1930s and 1940s, there were hundreds of steel mills in Ohio, Pennsylvania, and West Virginia. In her book* No Star Nights, *Anna Egan Smucker remembers what it was like to be a child in the mill town of Weirton, West Virginia. You have read part of this story on page 317 of your textbook. Now you can read more. What did the author's father do at the steel mill? How did manufacturing affect life in Weirton?*

When I was little, we couldn't see the stars in the nighttime sky because the furnaces of the mill turned the darkness into a red glow. But we would lie on the hill and look up at the sky anyway and wait for a bright orange light that seemed to breathe in and out to spread across it. And we would know that the golden spark-spitting steel was being poured out of giant buckets into molds to cool.

Then we would look down on a train pulling cars mounted with giant **thimbles** rocking back and forth. They were filled with fiery hot **molten slag** that in the night glowed orange. And when they were dumped, the sky lit up again.

**thimbles:** caps
**molten:** melted
**slag:** leftover materials

131

A loud steam whistle that echoed off the hills announced the change of shifts, and hundreds of men streamed out of the mill's gates. Everyone's dad worked in the mill, and carried a tin lunch box and a big metal thermos bottle.

Work at the mill went on night and day. When Dad worked night shift, we children had to whisper and play quietly during the day so that we didn't wake him up. His job was too dangerous for him to go without sleep. He operated a crane that lifted heavy **ingots** of steel into a pit that was thousands of degrees hot.

**ingots:** bars of metal

When Dad worked the **three-to-eleven** shift, Mom made dinner early so we could all eat together. She made the best stuffed cabbage of anyone in the neighborhood. We sometimes tried to help fold the cabbage leaves around the meat and rice like she did, but our cabbage leaves always came unrolled.

**three-to-eleven:** 3:00 P.M. to 11:00 P.M.

During the school year days went by when we didn't see Dad at all because he was either at work or sleeping. When he changed shifts from daylight to night and back again it took him a while to get used to the different waking and sleeping times. We called these his grumpy times. We liked it best when he had daylight hours to spend with us. We played baseball until it was too dark to see the ball.

On a few very special summer afternoons he would load us all into the car for a hot, sweaty trip to Pittsburgh and a double header Pirates game at Forbes Field. We sat in the bleachers way out in left field, eating popcorn and drinking lemonade that we brought from home, yelling our heads off for the Pirates. Our brother always wore his baseball glove, hoping to catch a foul ball that might come into the stands. Dad helped us mark our scorecards and bought us hot dogs during the seventh-inning stretch.

On our way home we passed the black **silhouettes** of Pittsburgh's steel mills with their great heavy clouds of

**silhouettes:** outlines

smoke **billowing** from endless rows of smokestacks. The road wound along as the river wound and between us and the river were the mills and on the other side of the road were the hills—the river, the mills, and the hills. And we sang as we rode home. "She'll be comin' round the mountain when she comes...."

We went to school across from the mill. The smokestacks towered above us and the smoke billowed out in great puffy clouds of red, orange, and yellow, but mostly the color of rust. Everything—houses, hedges, old cars—was a rusty red color. Everything but the little bits of **graphite** and they glinted like silver in the dust. At recess when the wind whirled these sharp shiny metal pieces around, we girls would crouch so that our skirts touched the ground and kept our bare legs from being stung.

We would squint our eyes when the wind blew to keep the graphite out. Once a piece got caught in my eye and no matter how much I blinked or how much my eye watered it wouldn't come out. When the eye doctor finally took it out and showed it to me I was amazed that a speck that small could feel so big.

We played on the steep street that ran up the hill beside our school. Our favorite game was dodge ball. The kids on the bottom row knew they had to catch the ball. If they didn't, it would roll down onto the busy county road that ran in front of the school. Too often a truck carrying a heavy roll of steel would run over it and with a loud bang the ball would be flattened.

The windows in our school were kept closed to try to keep the graphite and smoke out. On really windy days we could hear the dry, dusty sound of grit hitting against the glass. Dusting the room was a daily job. The best duster got to dust the teacher's desk with a soft white cloth and a spray that made the whole room smell like lemons. It was always a mystery to us how the nuns

**billowing:** blowing

**graphite:** a soft, gray mineral

who were our teachers could keep the white parts of their **habits** so clean....

**habits:** nuns' clothing

The road we took home from school went right through part of the mill. Tall cement walls with strands of barbed wire at the top kept us on the sidewalk and out of the mill. But when we got to the bridge that spanned the railroad tracks, there was just a steel mesh fence. From there we could look straight down into the mill! There was always something wonderful to watch. Through a huge open doorway we could see the **mammoth open-hearth** furnace. A giant **ladle** would tilt to give the fiery furnace a "drink" of orange, molten iron. Sometimes we would see the golden liquid steel pouring out the bottom of the open hearth into enormous bucketlike ladles. The workers were just small dark figures made even smaller by the great size of the ladles and the furnace. The hot glow of the liquid steel made the dark mill light up as if the sun itself was being poured out. And standing on the bridge we could feel its awful heat....

**mammoth:** huge
**open-hearth:** open at the front
**ladle:** spoon

Many years have passed since....The night sky is clear and star filled because the mill is shut down. The big buckets no longer pour the hot, yellow steel. The furnaces whose fires lit up everything are rusting and cold.

Not many children live in the town now. Most of the younger people have moved away to other places to find work. The valley's steelworking way of life is gone forever. But whenever the grandchildren come back to visit they love more than anything else to listen to stories about the days when all night long the sky glowed red.

*Just as in Weirton, many steel mills have closed down. How did the loss of industry change mill town communities? What types of work might have replaced steel manufacturing in these towns?*

Source: Anna Egan Smucker, *No Star Nights.* New York: Knopf, 1989.

# What a Wonderful World

## Song by George David Weiss and Bob Thiele

*As the world becomes more connected by people trading goods with each other, it is important that people share and appreciate nature. According to the lyrics of this song, what are some of nature's contributions to our "wonderful world"?*

I see trees of green, red roses too,
I see them bloom for me and you,
and I think to myself What a wonderful world.

I see skies of blue and clouds of white,
the bright blessed day, the dark sacred night,
and I think to myself What a wonderful world.

The colors of the rainbow, so pretty in the sky
are also on the faces of people goin' by,
I see friends shakin' hands, sayin', "How do you do!"
They're really sayin' "I love you,"

I hear babies cry, I watch them grow
They'll learn much more than I'll ever know
and I think to myself What a wonderful world.
Yes, I think to myself What a wonderful world.

*Do you think this is a song that people everywhere can appreciate? Why?*

Source: George David Weiss and Bob Thiele, *What a Wonderful World*. Range Road Music Inc. and Quartet Music Inc., 1967.

# INDEX BY *Category*

# INDEX BY *Title*

# ACKNOWLEDGMENTS

*(continued from copyright page)*

"The House on Hillside Lane" from ALDO APPLESAUCE by Johanna Hurwitz. Text ©1979 by Johanna Hurwitz. Morrow Junior Books, a division of William Morrow & Company, Inc.

"Field" from COUNTRY PIE by Frank Asch. ©1979 by Frank Asch. Greenwillow Books, a division of William Morrow & Company, Inc.

"City: San Francisco" and "Trip: San Francisco" by Langston Hughes. ©1958 by Langston Hughes. © renewed 1986 by George Houston Bass.

BEFORE YOU CAME THIS WAY by Byrd Baylor. ©1969 by Byrd Baylor. Penguin USA Inc.

WHERE THE RIVER BEGINS by Thomas Locker. ©1984 by Thomas Locker. Penguin USA Inc.

ALL THE PLACES TO LOVE by Patricia MacLachlan. Copyright ©1994 Patricia MacLachlan.

Excerpts from DEAR WORLD: HOW CHILDREN AROUND THE WORLD FEEL ABOUT OUR ENVIRONMENT. Edited by Lannis Temple. From DEAR WORLD by Lannis Temple. Copyright © 1992 by Lannis Temple. Reprinted by permission of Random House Inc.

Excerpts from ...IF YOU LIVED IN COLONIAL TIMES by Ann McGovern. ©1964 Ann McGovern. Four Winds Press, a division of Scholastic Magazines, Inc., NY.

Excerpt from EAGLE DRUM by Robert Crum. ©1994 Robert Crum. Four Winds Press, a division of Macmillan Publishing Company, NY.

Excerpt from EARTHQUAKE!: A STORY OF OLD SAN FRANCISCO by Kathleen V. Kudlinski. Text copyright © Kathleen V. Kudlinski, 1993. Reprinted by permission of Puffin Books, a division of Penguin Books USA, Inc.

Excerpt from MR. BLUE JEANS: A STORY ABOUT LEVI STRAUSS by Maryann N. Weidt. Text copyright © 1990 by Maryann N. Weidt. Reprinted by permission of Carolrhoda Books, Inc.

Excerpt from STRIKING IT RICH: THE STORY OF THE CALIFORNIA GOLD RUSH by Stephen Krensky. Text copyright © 1996 by Stephen Krensky. Reprinted by permission Simon & Schuster Books for Young Readers, an imprint of Simon & Schuster.

CITY GREEN by DyAnne DiSalvo-Ryan. Copyright ©1994 by DyAnne DiSalvo-Ryan. By permission of Morrow Junior Books, a division of William Morrow & Company, Inc.

Excerpts from DEAR MR. PRESIDENT: GREETINGS AND ADVICE TO A NEW LEADER FROM THE NATION'S YOUNGEST CITIZENS. Edited by Peggy Hackman and Don Oldenburg. ©1993 The Washington Post Co. Avon Books, a division of The Hearst Corporation, NY.

"Diary of Amelia Stewart Knight" from DIARY OF AN OREGON PIONEER OF 1853 by Amelia Stewart Knight. ©1928 Transactions of the Oregon Pioneer Association.

"When I First Came to This Land," Words and Music by Oscar Brand. TRO – © Copyright 1957 (Renewed) 1965 (Renewed) Ludlow Music, Inc., New York, NY. Used by Permission.

Excerpt from IMMIGRANT GIRL: BECKY OF ELDRIDGE STREET by Brett Harvey. Text copyright ©1987 by Brett Harvey. All rights reserved. Reprinted from IMMIGRANT GIRL: BECKY OF ELDRIDGE STREET by permission of Holiday House, Inc.

"Ancestry" from SING TO THE SUN by Ashley Bryan. Copyright ©1992 by Ashley Bryan.

Excerpt from HALMONI AND THE PICNIC by Sook Nyul Choi. ©1993 Sook Nyul Choi. Houghton Mifflin Company, NY.

From THE WRIGHT BROTHERS: HOW THEY INVENTED THE AIRPLANE by Russell Freedman. Reprinted by permission of Holiday House, Inc., from THE WRIGHT BROTHERS: HOW THEY INVENTED THE AIRPLANE copyright ©1991 by Russell Freedman.

Excerpt from THE FIRST RIDE: BLAZING THE TRAIL FOR THE PONY EXPRESS by Jacqueline Geis. ©1994 Jacqueline Geis. Ideals Children's Books, an imprint of Hambleton-Hill Publishing, Inc., TN.

"What a Wonderful World," Words and Music by George David Weiss and Bob Thiele. Copyright © 1967 by Range Road Music Inc. and Quartet Music Inc.

Excerpt from THE TOWN THAT MOVED by Mary Jane Finsand. ©1983 by Carolrhoda Books, Inc.

Excerpts from JAMESTOWN: NEW WORLD ADVENTURE by James E. Knight. ©1982 Troll Associates.

"No Star Nights" from NO STAR NIGHTS by Anna Egan Smucker. ©1989 by Anna Egan Smucker.

From UNCLE JED'S BARBERSHOP by Margaree King Marshall. ©1993 Simon & Schuster, NY.

# ACKNOWLEDGMENTS

"Children of Long Ago" from CHILDREN OF LONG AGO by Lessie Jones Little. Text copyright © 1988 by Weston Little. Reprinted by permission of Philomel Books. Recorded by permission of Marie Brown Associates.

IN COAL COUNTRY by Judith Hendershot. Copyright © 1987 by Judith Hendershot. Reprinted by permission of Random House Inc.

"Rise and Shine (Give Yourself a Chance)" by Professor Rap. Copyright © 1990 Professor Rap. Used by permission of Professor Rap.

"The City Blues" from FOLK BLUES by Jerry Silverman. Copyright © 1983 by Saw Mill Music, Inc. Used by permission of Saw Mill Music, Inc.

Excerpts from IF YOU LIVED AT THE TIME OF THE GREAT SAN FRANCISCO EARTHQUAKE by Ellen Levine. Copyright © 1987 by Ellen Levine. Reprinted by permission of Scholastic Inc.

Excerpts from IF YOU WERE THERE WHEN THEY SIGNED THE CONSTITUTION by Elizabeth Levy. Copyright © 1987 by Elizabeth Levy. Reprinted by permission of of Scholastic Inc.

Excerpts from MY BEST FRIEND MEE-YUNG KIM *Meeting a Korean-American Family* by Dianne MacMillan and Dorothy Freeman. Copyright © 1989 by Dianne MacMillan and Dorothy Freeman. Reprinted by permission of Simon & Schuster.

Taken from the book *50 Simple Things Kids Can Do to Save the Earth* by John Javna. Copyright © 1990 by John Javna. Reprinted by permission of Andrews & McMeel. All rights reserved.

MUSIC, MUSIC FOR EVERYONE by Vera B. Williams. Copyright © 1984 by Vera B. Williams. By permission of Greenwillow Books, a division of William Morrow & Company, Inc.

Excerpt from JOHN HENRY: An American Legend by Ezra Jack Keats. Text copyright © 1965 by Ezra Jack Keats. Abridgement by arrangement with Alfred A. Knopf, Inc. Recorded by arrangement with Alfred A. Knopf.

Excerpt from THE PATCHWORK QUILT by Valerie Flournoy. Copyright © 1985 by Valerie Flournoy for text, copyright © 1985 by Jerry Pinkney for pictures. Used by permission.

Excerpt from YAGUA DAYS by Cruz Martel. Text copyright © 1976 by Cruz Martel. Reprinted by permission of Penguin USA.

## CREDITS

**Photography:** 120: Courtesy of Brian Massie. 121: t. Courtesy of Denice Burnham; b. Courtesy of Leon Harris.

**Cover:** Pentagram.

**Illustration:** Michael David Biegel, 36, 38, 40, 54, 59; John Bowdren 60; Susan Dodge 10; Grace Goldberg 11–13, 22, 23, 24, 41, 42, 43, 71, 72, 75; James Grashow 128; Janet Hamlin 44, 50, 95, 122; Marcie Hawthorne 2, 3, 5; Meryl Henderson 6, 9; Fiona King 76, 77, 108, 109, 112; Dan Krovatin 96, 97; Richard Leonard 91–94, Laurie Marks 131, 133, 134; Jim McConnell 87, 126; Ife Nii-Owoo 66–70, 129, 130; Marty Norman 103, 104, 105, 106, 107; Vilma Ortiz 32–35; Marcy Ramsey 78, 82, 100, 101; Cecil Rice 29, 31; Lauren Rosenblum 61–65; Doug Roy 26–28; Dennis Schofield 84, 86, 89, 90.

# TEACHING *Strategies*

Teachers share a common goal—to help their students become successful learners who can understand, remember, and apply important knowledge and skills. This important goal is best supported when students are offered a variety of ways in which to learn.

The Social Studies Anthology offers you the rich and varied tools that you need to help your students learn. It includes such diverse sources as diaries, poems, songs, stories, legends, plays, and posters — all of which draw students into the sights and sounds of the places and times they are studying.

You may invite students to explore the Anthology selections in many unique ways—rewriting documents in another genre, dramatizing the selection, creating posters or collages, or writing original poems, stories, and songs. We have provided a strategy for teaching each selection in the Anthology. But these strategies, of course, are only suggestions. You should feel free to teach the selections in any way that you feel is best suited for your own classroom.

A Cassette accompanies the Social Studies Anthology and provides additional support in teaching the documents. Sometimes the recordings reproduce the voices of the people who wrote the selections. A Cassette logo lets you know which selections have been recorded.

# THE TOWN THAT MOVED
**by Mary Jane Finsand**
**Pages 2–5**

*Use with Chapter 1, Lesson 1*

## Objectives

☐ *Recognize that communities are often established where work or resources exist.*

☐ *Identify the ways in which the people of a community can work together to solve a problem.*

☐ *Write a newspaper article about the town that moved.*

### Writing a Newspaper Article

After students have read the selection, discuss with them why the town of Hibbing grew up where it did. (Iron ore had been discovered in the area, and people moved there to work in the mines.)

*What happened as the town grew?* (The town became more beautiful as hotels, parks, and lovely houses were built.) *What problem did the town eventually face?* (The best iron ore was located right under the town.) *How did the people of the community solve their problem?* (They worked with the mine owners to come up with a plan to move the town.)

Invite students to write a newspaper article about the town that moved. Remind students to answer *who, what, when, where, why,* and *how* in their articles.

# ALL THE PLACES TO LOVE
**by Patricia MacLachlan**
**Pages 6–9** 🔲

*Use with Chapter 1, Lesson 2*

## Objectives

☐ *Identify how the poet uses language to describe places in the country.*

☐ *Appreciate the beauties of rural areas.*

☐ *Write a poem from the perspective of a city dweller.*

### Exploring Perspectives

After students have read the poem, play it for them on the cassette. Discuss with students the images that the poet has created. *Which is their favorite image?* (Answers will vary.) *Why did Grandmother hold the newborn child up in the open window?* (so that she could see all the places to love) *What does the family think of where they live?* (They love the valleys and rivers and the hilltop where the blackberries grow.) *What other things are special to the family about the area?* (the meadows and fields, the animals and birds, the flowers, the barn) *What does Eli intend to do for his little sister?* (show her all the things to love that his family showed him)

Invite students to write a poem or a story from the perspective of someone who lives in the city. Before students write, you may wish to have the whole class brainstorm some things to love about cities. Record students' suggestions on the chalkboard so that students can refer to them when they write.

# CITY POEMS
**by Langston Hughes**
**Page 10** 🔲

*Use with Chapter 1, Lesson 2*

## Objectives

☐ *Name those details in the poems that could describe any city and those details that are especially descriptive of San Francisco.*

☐ *List special features about one's own community.*

☐ *Write a poem about the student's own community.*

## Writing a Poem

Have students read along as they listen to the poems on the cassette. Then ask volunteers to read the poems aloud to the class. Discuss which details in these poems could be about any city and which are especially descriptive of San Francisco. (Most cities have stone buildings and night lights; many have bridges, but this is a feature of special importance to San Francisco.)

Have students prepare to write poems about their community. Begin by asking each student to make a list of community features that would be most important to include in their poems. Then have them use some of these features to describe their community in the poems. They may wish either to follow the pattern of Hughes's poems or to write different kinds of poems altogether. Some students may wish to illustrate their poems with their own drawings. Have volunteers share their poems with the class.

# THE HOUSE ON HILLSIDE LA
**by Johanna Hurwitz**
**Pages 11–13**

*Use with Chapter 1, Lesson 2*

## Objectives

☐ *Recognize how the author reveals the different emotions that parents and children might feel about moving to a new community, school, or job.*

☐ *Hypothesize about events on Aldo's first day at his new school.*

☐ *Write a story about Aldo's first day in the Woodside School.*

## Writing a Story

After students have read the story, ask them why the family is moving. (father changing his job) Ask students to speculate about how the father may feel about the move to a new community. *How do the children feel?* (excited, tense, nervous) Ask if any students in the class have ever moved to a new community. Have volunteers share their experiences as the "new kid." Have others tell how they reacted to a new girl or boy who came into their class or neighborhood.

Ask students what they think will happen the next day when Aldo goes to school. Then have them write a story about Aldo's first day in his new school. Some students may wish to illustrate their stories and display them on the bulletin board.

# THE CITY BLUES
**American Folk Blues**
**Page 14** 🔲

---

*Use with Chapter 1, Lesson 2*

---

## Objectives

- ☐ *Locate the cities mentioned in the song on a map of the United States.*
- ☐ *Identify how the song links each city to a particular main feature.*
- ☐ *Build knowledge of the cities named in the song by doing small-group research.*

## Building Knowledge

Have students read the words of the song as they listen to it on the cassette. Then give them a chance to sing along as you play the cassette a second time. Afterward, using a map of the United States, have them locate the cities mentioned in the song. Tell them that a city sometimes acquires a nickname based on its most striking feature. Ask students if they know any such nicknames. (For example, Chicago is called "The Windy City.") Then have them name the one feature given for each city in the song. (the subway in New York, pecan pralines in New Orleans, and so on) If any students have visited any of the cities, ask if the feature mentioned in the song is something that they also observed in that city.

Divide the class into small groups, one for each city in the song. Provide them with travel brochures, if possible, or with an encyclopedia to learn more about the city. Tell students to think about this question: *If you had to pick a special feature to represent this city, would it be the one mentioned in the song?* Have members of each group write on the chalkboard the one or two prominent features they discovered about the city they researched.

# WHERE THE RIVER BEGINS
**by Thomas Locker**
**Pages 15–17**

---

*Use with Chapter 2, Lesson 1*

---

## Objectives

- ☐ *Identify examples of landforms in the story.*
- ☐ *Rewrite the story in the form of a diary entry written from the point of view of one of the boys.*

## Rewriting in Another Genre

After they have read the story, ask students to identify the landforms that the boys saw during their trip. Then discuss why they think Josh and Aaron wanted to find the place where the river begins. *Do you think the boys were satisfied with what they found?* (excited at first, satisfied at the sight of the peaceful pond, surprised at the sudden storm, impressed at how quickly the stream became flooded with rainwater)

Have students suppose that they are Josh or Aaron and write two or three diary entries about the camping trip to the source of the river. They should describe the way the river changed during the two-day trip.

# FIELD
**by Frank Asch**
**Page 18** 🔲

*Use with Chapter 1, Lesson 2*

## Objectives

- ❏ *Identify the author's point of view about suburban lawns.*
- ❏ *Write a response to the author's attitude toward fields and lawns.*

### Writing a Response

After students have read the poem, have them listen to it on the cassette. Then ask volunteers to read the poem aloud to the class. Have students list some of the things that the author liked about the field before it was a lawn. Ask if students have ever known a place that used to be wild or untended and has now been developed. (perhaps the site of a new shopping area, a new medical building, or new houses) Ask if they preferred the place before or after. Have them consider what might be some of the benefits of building new buildings, even if it means the loss of a natural area.

Have students try to determine the author's point of view about suburban lawns. Have them look for key words that are clues to his viewpoint, such as *just a lawn.* Then have students write a response to Frank Asch. They can either support or oppose his point of view about suburban lawns.

# DEAR WORLD
**edited by Lannis Temple**
**Pages 19–20**

*Use with Chapter 2, Lesson 2*

## Objectives

- ❏ *Recognize some of the characteristics of our planet's geography.*
- ❏ *Identify some things that we can do to protect our environment.*
- ❏ *Write a letter about the environment.*

### Writing a Letter

After students have read the selection, encourage them to discuss where the letter writers live. (the Netherlands, Japan, the United States, the West Bank) Help students to locate these places on a World map. Then ask students what the letters have in common. (They express what the writers like about the environment and enjoy in nature, and their concerns about protecting it.) *What do the writers enjoy about nature?* (oceans, beaches, mountains, meadows) *What concerns do they have?* (water and air pollution, damage to the ozone layer) Encourage students to discuss some of the geographical characteristics of where they live and what they enjoy about the geography of their area. Invite students to comment on any concerns they have about protecting the environment in their area.

Then suggest that students write their own letters to the people of the world. In their letters they should mention what they appreciate about nature and what they would do to protect it.

## 50 SIMPLE THINGS KIDS CAN DO TO RECYCLE
**by John Javna and The EarthWorks Group**
**Pages 21–24**

*Use with Chapter 2, Lesson 2*

### Objectives
- ❏ *Identify ways in which people can recycle glass and newspapers.*
- ❏ *Recognize the advantages of recycling.*
- ❏ *Create a poster showing ways to recycle.*

### Creating a Poster

After students have read the selection, discuss some of the facts they learned about recycling glass and newspapers. *Which facts surprised you most?* Help students come up with a definition for the word *recycle* (use something again, sometimes making it into something else) and discuss some of the specific recycling tips offered in the selection. (how to clean glass, how to bundle up newspapers) Then, ask students to talk about what might happen if we don't recycle. (We would deplete more raw materials, use more energy, create more waste.)

Have students create posters that show ways to recycle and list the benefits of recycling. They might depict a family bundling up newspapers or collecting glass. Display the completed posters around the classroom or, if possible, in school hallways.

## WHY WE HAVE DOGS IN HOPI VILLAGES
**Told to Byrd Baylor by Hopi Indian Children**
**Pages 26–28**

*Use with Chapter 3, Lesson 1*

### Objectives
- ❏ *Identify how the story focuses on ways to resolve conflicts in a group.*
- ❏ *Write a story to explain how something came to be.*

### Writing a Story

After students have read the story, ask them to describe what life was like in the village before the boy went on his journey. *What kinds of things might people have argued and fussed over?* Have students discuss how the village of dogs went about considering the boy's proposal. (invited him to a meeting of the chief and the council, allowed each dog to accept or reject the boy's invitation) *How did this help to prevent quarreling?* (allowed free discussion of issues and individual decisions)

Ask students if they have ever observed arguments within a group. Have them list ways that people can work to end conflicts within a group. (for example, taking the argument to a neutral third person, each party agreeing to compromise, one party leaving the group, all parties learning to understand and respect differences) *How did the boy try to stop the arguing?* (by getting dogs who didn't argue to come and live with his people)

Have students write another story about the boy in this tale. Have them tell how he solves another problem.

# EAGLE DRUM
## by Robert Crum
### Pages 29–31

*Use with Chapter 3, Lesson 1 and Legacy*

## Objectives

- [ ] *Identify the powwow as part of the Native American cultural heritage.*
- [ ] *Appreciate some of the customs associated with powwows.*
- [ ] *Write an interview of a powwow participant.*

## Writing an Interview

After students have read the selection, discuss with them the part dancing plays in the powwow. (Dancers engage in contests at the powwows; even though powwows have different dances and customs, there are many similarities so that dancers feel comfortable and welcome at the powwows.) *Why do David and Louis listen to the powwow songs?* (They put them in the spirit of the powwow and prepare them for the contest.) *Why is it important to have good thoughts in the dance arbor?* (The dancers believe that the good thoughts come back to you.) *What happened to the dancer who danced for the old man?* (It was the best night of dancing he ever had, the old man felt good, and his wife fixed the young dancer a good breakfast.)

Have students think of some questions they would like to ask a participant in the powwow. Students should try to come up with five questions and possible answers. Partners can act out the interviews for the class.

# BEFORE YOU CAME THIS WAY
## by Byrd Baylor
### Pages 32–35

*Use with Chapter 3, Lesson 4*

## Objectives

- [ ] *Appreciate how Byrd Baylor describes the accomplishments of the Anasazi.*
- [ ] *List the strengths and weaknesses of communicating through pictures.*
- [ ] *Create graphics for personal versions of rock paintings.*

## Background

In the 900s B.C. the cultural and religious center of the Anasazi was Chaco, in what is now New Mexico. Miles of road fanned out from the city in every direction, connecting Chaco to scattered villages and sources of trade goods. People came from as far away as Mexico to trade beans, corn, copper, pottery, macaws, and turquoise. Hundreds of people lived in each of the 13 separate villages that made up the city of Chaco. Thousands of others journeyed there, including merchants, artisans, and people on religious pilgrimages. Today people can visit Chaco Culture National Historic Park and its largest pueblo, *Pueblo Bonito* ("Beautiful Village"), to glimpse the architectural ruins and *almost* capture the sounds and sights of the ancient city.

## Creating Graphics

After students have read the poem, play the recording on the cassette for them. Suggest to students that they close their eyes and try to picture the images created by the poem as they listen to it. Have them examine and discuss the pictures of Anasazi architecture and rock paintings. Ask students how they think archaeologists are able to decipher the clues they uncover.

Suggest to students that they make their own drawings of key events and places they remember or have read about. The drawings should be simple and in a style that could be carved in stone. After students have drawn two or three scenes or events, have them trade papers with a partner and try to decipher each other's work. Discuss the strengths and weaknesses of communicating through pictures.

# JAMESTOWN: NEW WORLD ADVENTURE
**by James E. Knight**
**Pages 36–40**

*Use with Chapter 4, Lesson 2*

## Objectives

- ☐ *Recognize the hardships faced by the Jamestown settlers.*
- ☐ *Identify ways in which early settlers interacted with Native Americans to meet their needs.*
- ☐ *Write a journal entry about life in Jamestown.*

### Writing a Journal Entry

After students have read the selection, discuss with them what life was like in the Jamestown settlement according to this fact-based, fictional journal. (Life was very difficult—the land had to be cleared, food had to be secured, relationships with the Native Americans had to be forged, and diseases had to be overcome.) *How did the Native Americans help the settlers?* (Powhatan gave the settlers corn and other goods.) *What happened when John Smith was injured and had to return to England?* (Relationships with the Native Americans broke down, and they would no longer supply food.) *What happened to the settlement at Jamestown?* (It survived, but many died from the hardships of living there.)

Have students write another journal entry about life in Jamestown. Students can use the selection, their social studies text, or other reference materials to get ideas for their entry. Encourage students to share their entries with the class.

# ...IF YOU LIVED IN COLONIAL TIMES
**by Ann McGovern**
**Pages 41–43**

*Use with Chapter 4, Lesson 2*

## Objectives

- ☐ *Identify some characteristics of life during colonial times.*
- ☐ *Write a story about what it would have been like to be a child in colonial times.*

### Rewriting in Another Genre

After students have read the selection, ask them to discuss what life was like for children during colonial times. *What rules did children have to follow?* (Students may quote rules from first page of selection.) *What was education like for children in colonial times?* (Boys and girls went to a Dame School; then boys went on to another school and girls learned at home.) *What did children learn at the Dame School?* (how to read and write) *What were the schools like?* (They were not comfortable; students did not have many books or supplies; most boys stopped school at age 11.)

Invite students to write a story about what it would have been like to be a child going to school in colonial times. You may wish to have partners work together to write a story. Students can share their stories with the class.

# IN GOOD OLD COLONY TIMES
**American Ballad**
**Page 44** 🎵

*Use with Chapter 4, Lesson 2*

## Objectives

☐ *Identify how the ballad entertains at the same time that it tells a story.*

☐ *Recognize that ballads and folk songs traveled by word of mouth during our country's early history.*

☐ *Write a ballad.*

## Writing a Ballad

After students have read the words to the ballad, play the song for them on the cassette. Then play it a second time, so they can join in on the refrains.

Remind students that ballads and folk songs could serve as sources of news, information, gossip, or entertainment. These songs often traveled by word of mouth before they were ever written down. Ask students if they know of any examples of songs that are spread in this way today. (jump-rope songs, hand-clapping songs, funny versions of regular songs)

Suggest to students that they use the tune of "In Good Old Colony Times" and write lyrics to create a ballad of their own. Volunteers may sing their songs or make a tape to play for the class. Have the class compare the students' ballads with "In Good Old Colony Times." *Do they also tell stories in an entertaining way?*

# STRIKING IT RICH: THE STORY OF THE CALIFORNIA GOLD RUSH
**by Stephen Krensky**
**Pages 45–46**

*Use with Chapter 5, Lesson 2*

## Objectives

☐ *Recognize how news can be exaggerated.*

☐ *Write a letter that explains the decisions one might make when faced with the possibility of a quick fortune.*

## Writing a Letter

After the students have read the story, discuss with them how facts can be easily exaggerated when passed on by word of mouth, especially when it is something that people would like to believe is true.

Have the students imagine that they are living and working in San Francisco in 1848 when news of gold comes their way. They have a good job, but they are thinking about leaving it to hunt for gold. Have them write a letter to a relative in the east that explains what they plan to do and why. Do they want to quit their job and risk not finding any gold? Would they encourage their relative to move to San Francisco and hunt for gold too? If they did want their relative to move out West, why might they exaggerate the claims of "striking it rich"?

Ask students to read each other's letters and pretend that they are the relatives to whom the letters were written. Would the letters make them want to head out for San Francisco?

# MR. BLUE JEANS: A STORY ABOUT LEVI STRAUSS

**by Maryann N. Weidt**
**Pages 47–48**

*Use with Chapter 5, Lesson 2*

## Objectives

❏ *Recognize that to be successful in business it helps to understand and appreciate the needs of the people around you.*

❏ *Create an advertisement that demonstrates an understanding of what life was probably like for gold miners.*

### Create an Advertisement

When gold was discovered in California in 1848, many people came in search of fortune. Point out to students that this created many new businesses of providing goods and services to the people mining for gold. After the students have read the selection, discuss how Levi Strauss became successful by providing a new product that suited the miners' particular needs. If Levi wanted to sell even more pants during the goldrush by advertising in newspapers, what might his ad say?

Have students write and illustrate an advertisment for a product that would have been popular during the gold rush. Point out that students should think about the kinds of qualities that gold miners would want in their purchases. (easy to carry, durable, makes camping easier and more pleasant) Levi was paid six dollars in gold dust for his pants. Ask students how much they would charge for their products.

# EARTHQUAKE!

**By Kathleen V. Kudlinski**
**Pages 49–52**

*Use with Chapter 5, Lesson 2*

## Objectives

❏ *Evaluate how the main character of the story handled an emergency situation.*

❏ *Identify the importance of planning ahead for an emergency.*

❏ *Make a plan for a course of action during an emergency.*

### Making an Emergency Plan

After the students have read the selection, discuss how Phillip handled the emergency. Did he act responsibly? (Yes, he put out the fire and tried to fill up the trough with water before he left the stable). How was he prepared for this emergency? (He had practiced what to do in the event of a barn fire and had water in the trough.)

Ask students about what kind of emergency situations they might some day encounter during an earthquake. Discuss what kinds of steps should be taken before and during such an emergency. (In the event of a fire, students should consider fire drills, escape routes, fire alarms, avoiding smoke and flames.) Have students write and illustrate their emergency plan. How would emergency plans today differ from those of Phillip's time?

# BEN AND BOOKS
by Navidad O'Neill
Pages 54–59

Use with Chapter 6, Lesson 1

## Objectives

- [ ] *Recognize that the play entertains as well as provides information about the accomplishments of Benjamin Franklin.*
- [ ] *Identify some of the contributions Benjamin Franklin made to our country.*
- [ ] *Perform a Readers Theater version of the play.*

## Using Readers Theater

After students have read the play, discuss with students why it is a good idea to have six Bens. (Benjamin Franklin accomplished a great deal; having six Bens gives more students a chance to play the part.) Then encourage students to name some of Franklin's specific accomplishments. (He was a great thinker, inventor, statesman, and writer.)

Choose students to play the parts in the play. Tell students that their performance will make use only of the spoken word, but before they begin they might wish to picture what the setting and costumes might look like if they were actually producing the play in a theater. Arrange the six Bens in chairs in front of the class. As they read, remind them that they will have to convey their character's feelings solely through the way they speak their lines, since there is no action in this type of presentation. Suggest to them that they can make their characters real through changes in tone of voice, volume, and so on. The chorus can sit on the floor around the six Bens. After readers have practiced their lines, perform the Readers Theater for the classroom or another class.

# WASHINGTON THE GREAT
Traditional American Song
Page 60

Use with Chapter 6, Lesson 2

## Objectives

- [ ] *Identify how the song entertains as well as provides information about George Washington.*
- [ ] *Write another verse for the song.*

## Writing a Song Verse

After students have read the lyrics to the song, play the song for them on the cassette or on the piano if you have access to one. Invite students to sing along.

Discuss with students some of the things they learned about George Washington from the song. Then have students write another verse for the song. Students can use information from the song or other information about Washington that they know. When students are satisfied with their verses, they may wish to sing them for the class.

# . . . IF YOU WERE THERE WHEN THEY SIGNED THE CONSTITUTION
by Elizabeth Levy
Pages 61–65

Use with Chapter 6, Lesson 2

## Objectives

- ☐ Name the current President, your state's Senators, and your district's Representative in Congress.
- ☐ Identify the steps described in this selection for making a new law.
- ☐ Write an account of the making of a new law.

### Rewriting in Another Genre

After students read the selection, ask them: *Can you name the President of the United States? Do you know who represents us in the Senate and House of Representatives?* (You might tell them the answers if they don't know them, or you might choose students to research the answers.)

Help students to understand the process by which a bill becomes a law. You might draw a flow chart on the chalkboard, illustrating the information presented in this selection. Then have students think of a law they would like to see passed by Congress. Have them write an account of the steps that would be needed to get that law passed. You might choose one student's account to flesh out as a "Model Congress" activity so that the class can experience the lawmaking process.

# WHAT ARE YOU FIGURING NOW?
by Jeri Ferris
Pages 66–70

Use with Chapter 7, Lesson 1

## Objectives

- ☐ Identify the skills described in this biography that made Banneker a good surveyor's chief assistant.
- ☐ Locate Washington, D.C., on a map of the United States, and measure the distance between the capital and your community.
- ☐ Write a journal entry from Banneker's perspective about mapping out Washington, D.C.

### Exploring Perspectives

After students have read the story, list the skills that Banneker needed to be the chief surveyor's chief assistant. (had to know how to use a telescope, an astronomical clock, and surveyor's tools; had to be able to do calculations) Discuss how Banneker might have felt during the months he spent mapping out the plans for Washington, D.C. (for example, excited, proud, tired, cold, competent)

Have the class locate Washington, D.C., on a map of the United States. Help them to find your community on the map and to compare the two locations in terms of such things as nearness to oceans and rivers and to other geographical features of the country. Then ask them to calculate the approximate distance between Washington and your community.

Have students suppose that they are Benjamin Banneker. Then ask them: *What do you think about the new city and about your work in getting it ready?* Have students write one or more journal entries from Banneker's perspective about Washington, D.C., and about his contribution to it.

# CITY GREEN
**by DyAnne DiSalvo-Ryan**
**Pages 71–75**

*Use with Chapter 8, Lessons 1 and 2*

## Objectives

- ❏ *Identify the part citizens play in improving their community.*
- ❏ *Recognize what can be accomplished when members of the community understand their local government.*
- ❏ *Build citizenship by illustrating how people can make a difference.*

## Building Citizenship

After students have read the selection, have them discuss what happened to the building in the neighborhood. (It was torn down because it was unsafe.) *How did the people of the neighborhood feel about the building being torn down?* (They were upset because now there was an unattractive empty lot there.) *What do Miss Rosa and Marcy decide to do?* (They want to make a garden on the empty lot; they investigate the possibility with a neighbor who used to work with the city.) *What are they able to accomplish?* (For a fee of one dollar, the city lets them use the lot to grow a garden.) *What does Mr. Hammer finally do?* (He plants some sunflowers in the lot and they grow to be the tallest and prettiest in the garden; he enjoys the garden every day at lunchtime and sometimes at dinnertime.)

Invite students to come up with a plan to improve an area in their community. It could be an empty lot or a street that needs some care. Students should work in small groups to set a goal and come up with a plan. Students can then share their plans with the class.

# DEAR MR. PRESIDENT
**Letters to the *Washington Post***
**Pages 76–77**

*Use with Chapter 7, Lesson 2, and Chapter 8, Lesson 2*

## Objectives

- ❏ *Recognize that the voice of each citizen is important in a democracy.*
- ❏ *Identify the role of the President of the United States.*
- ❏ *Conduct an interview with the President of the United States.*

## Conducting an Interview

After students have read the selection, discuss with them some of the points raised in the letters to the President. Then ask students why it is important to let government officials know what you think about issues. (Government officials are elected representatives of the people; they need to know how the people feel about things.) Then discuss with students what the role of the President is in our country. (He is the leader and the commander in chief; it is important that the President listen to the people he serves.)

Have students think of some questions they would like to ask the President if they could interview him. Each student should try to come up with two questions. Then the whole class can review the questions and select ten of them. The class can tape-record the questions and send them to the President.

# JULIO IN THE LION'S DEN

**by Johanna Hurwitz**
**Pages 78–82**

*Use with Chapter 8, Lesson 2*

## Objectives

☐ *Identify ways in which the story is realistic.*

☐ *Describe features of a good campaign for class president.*

☐ *Write a story telling what happened next in the campaign for president in Julio's class.*

### Writing Your Own Story

After students have read the selection, have them discuss the ways in which the story told is realistic. Ask students: *What issue at your school might cause you to request a meeting with the principal? What arguments would you make to convince the principal of your point of view? Whom would you choose to go with you to talk with him or her? Why?* Then have students discuss whether Cricket was running a good campaign for president. Ask: *What should Lucas have done to campaign against her?* (Accept all reasonable answers.)

Have students think about who might win the election for president of Julio's class. Then have them write the next part of the story, telling about the rest of the campaign and the election. Ask volunteers to share their endings with the class.

# DIARY OF MRS. AMELIA STEWART KNIGHT

**by Amelia Stewart Knight**
**Pages 84–86**

*Use with Chapter 9, Lesson 1*

## Objectives

☐ *Recognize the selection as a primary source.*

☐ *Identify the hardships faced by travelers on the Oregon Trail.*

☐ *Write a diary entry about life on the Oregon Trail.*

### Writing a Diary Entry

After students have read the selection, encourage them to define a primary source and to explain why primary sources are valuable to our study of history. (A primary source is an account of an event written by someone who was actually there. Primary sources are valuable because they give us firsthand information about a particular time in history.) Then encourage students to discuss the kinds of hardships travelers on the Oregon Trail faced. (uncertainties of weather, food, river crossings, and so on) *What kinds of people were these new settlers? Why did they wish to start new communities in the West?* (Responses will vary, but should address the notion that the new settlers were courageous people, who wished to settle new communities in hopes of improving their lives.)

Invite students to write a diary entry for the day that Amelia Stewart Knight arrived in Oregon. *How did the family feel on that day? What did they do?* Students may wish to share their diary entries in small groups or read them to the class.

# WHEN I FIRST CAME TO THIS LAND

**by Oscar Brand**
**Page 87** 🎵

---

*Use with Chapter 9, Lesson 2*

## Objectives

- [ ] *Recognize that the song entertains as well as describes the life of a new arrival in this country.*
- [ ] *Identify some of the difficulties new immigrants face.*
- [ ] *Write a story about an immigrant family.*

### Writing a Story

After students have read the lyrics to the song, play the song for them on the cassette or on a piano if you have access to one. Then play the song a second time and invite students to sing along. Encourage students to discuss the initial run of bad luck described in the song. *Do you think this sort of thing actually happened to new arrivals?* (song may exaggerate for humor, but is probably based on real experiences) Then ask students to speculate about why, throughout it all, "the land was sweet and good." (Immigrants were willing to endure hardships because of a chance at improving their lives.)

Have students write a story about the family in the song. You may wish to brainstorm ideas with the whole class before students begin their stories. Encourage students to think about what happens to the family after the last verse of the song.

# IMMIGRANT GIRL

**by Brett Harvey**
**Pages 88–90**

---

*Use with Chapter 9, Lesson 2*

## Objectives

- [ ] *Identify how immigrants adopt the customs of their new country and retain some of their old ones as well.*
- [ ] *Recognize the hardships that immigrant families faced.*
- [ ] *Write a report about immigration during the early 1900s.*

### Writing a Report

After students have read the selection, discuss with them why the family left Russia. (They were being persecuted in Russia for their religion.) *Where does the family live now?* (They live in New York City on the Lower East Side.) *What are some of the customs that the family has retained from their life in Russia?* (speaking Yiddish, eating some of the foods) *What are some of the customs of their new land that they have adopted?* (They are learning English; they go to the movies; they play games in the street.) Then ask students to discuss some of the hardships that immigrants faced. (learning a new language, finding work, fitting in to a new country, and so on) Point out to students that many immigrants came to the United States in the early 1900s.

Invite students to conduct some library research about the immigrants who came to this country in the early 1900s. They can use the encyclopedia or other reference books. Encourage students to write two or three paragraphs. Students can share their reports with the class.

# CHILDTIMES
## by Eloise Greenfield and Lessie Jones Little
### Pages 91–94

---

*Use with Chapter 10, Lesson 1*

## Objectives

- ❏ *Recognize how each woman's account reflects the changes she witnessed in her hometown as she grew up.*
- ❏ *Identify ways that families stayed the same as the town changed.*
- ❏ *Rewrite the selection as a conversation among the three women.*

## Rewriting in Another Genre

After students have read *Childtimes*, discuss how the town of Parmele changed and became almost three different towns over three generations. *In the grandmother's day, what changed Parmele into a boom town?* (People came to work in the lumber mill.) *What change had occurred in Parmele by the time the daughter was growing up?* (The lumber mill had closed down and many people had left.) *Why did the granddaughter's family continue to visit the town?* (to see friends and relatives)

Have students think about what the three women would say if they could sit down and talk about life in Parmele. Have students write a conversation that might take place among the three. Then let trios of students read the conversations aloud for the class.

# ANCESTRY
## by Ashley Bryan
### Page 95 📼

---

*Use with Chapter 9, Lesson 3*

## Objectives

- ❏ *Recognize how the poet uses language to describe the importance of heritage to a young boy.*
- ❏ *Interview someone about his or her ancestry.*

## Conducting an Interview

After students have read the poem, take an opportunity to read it aloud. You may wish to read the poem or call upon volunteers to do so. Ask students to think about the images in the poem. *What is the scene described in the poem?* (Children are playing on the beach.) *What do the parents in the poem do?* (They tell their children stories about where their ancestors came from.) Have students provide a definition for the word *ancestor*. (relative from long ago) *Why is it important to know about our ancestors?* (so we have a sense of our past and our family's past) *What is the ancestry of the child in the poem?* (African)

Invite students to interview someone about his or her ancestry. You may wish to invite a guest or two to class to answer students' questions, or you may wish to assign the interview as homework and have students interview a person of their choice. In either case, ask students to come up with a list of questions they would like to ask the person they will interview. Students can brainstorm questions in small groups. When the interviews are complete invite students to share their findings with the class. You may wish to hold a follow-up discussion about the meaning of ancestry.

# HALMONI AND THE PICNIC
by Sook Nyul Choi
Pages 96–99

*Use with Chapter 9, Lesson 4*

## Objectives

- ❑ *Recognize the contributions that immigrant groups make to our culture.*
- ❑ *Identify some aspects of Korean culture.*
- ❑ *Create a book of recipes for the class.*

## Creating a Book

After students have read the selection, discuss what the children at the picnic learned from Halmoni. *What did Halmoni wear to the picnic? What food did she bring? What language did she speak?* (Halmoni wore traditional Korean clothing—a ch'ima and chigori with white pointed shoes; she brought a traditional dish—kimbap; she spoke Korean.) Ask students what made Halmoni feel good at the picnic. (She felt good when the children liked the food she brought and when they asked her to hold the jump rope and used the name of her food in the jump rope rhyme.) *Do you think Halmoni will go to the picnic next year?* (Responses will vary, but should get at the notion that probably Halmoni will go to the picnic because she had a good time this year.) *Do you think she will know more English?* (Yes, because she will have been in the United States a year longer.) Point out that when immigrants come to our country, they bring with them many traditions, such as food, music, dancing, games and that those traditions become part of ours country's traditions.

Invite students to create a book of "Foods from Different Lands" for the class. Students might bring recipes from home that come from their particular culture, and they can do some research on foods from other lands. Students can glue their recipes to construction paper, three-hole punch the construction paper, and bind the recipes together using yarn.

# IN A NEIGHBORHOOD IN LOS ANGELES
by Francisco X. Alarcón
Pages 100–101

*Use with Chapter 9, Lesson 4*

## Objectives

- ❑ *Identify some of the cultural elements of Mexico that were passed on to the poet by his grandmother.*
- ❑ *List other ways that culture and traditions can be passed on.*
- ❑ *Write a paragraph about the poet's grandmother.*

## Building Citizenship

Point out to students that the poet has chosen to present his poem using few capital letters and no punctuation marks. Have them listen to the cassette to see how the reader groups the individual thoughts and ideas. If anyone in the class speaks Spanish, have one student read the poem aloud in Spanish and another read it aloud in English.

After students have listened to and read the poem, discuss the important role of the grandmother in passing along Mexican traditions to her grandson. *In what ways did he learn about Mexico from her?* (She spoke Spanish to him, performed Mexican songs and dances for him, and described Mexico to him.) *In what other ways can culture be passed on to children?* (for example, by practicing religious customs; by taking part in traditional family celebrations and community events)

Remind students that immigrants make important contributions to their new communities. Have students write a paragraph about the poet's grandmother. The paragraph should describe her contribution to the preservation of Mexican culture. Ask volunteers to share their paragraphs with the class.

# SUCCESS
**Telegram Sent by Orville Wright**
**Page 102**

---

*Use with Chapter 10, Lessons 1 and 2*

## Objectives

☐ *Recognize the historical significance of the first airplane flight.*

☐ *Link the significance of the first flight to the significance of United States space exploration.*

### Linking to Today

After students have read the telegram, discuss with them the significance of the Wright brothers' accomplishment. *How did the invention of the airplane affect society?* (The invention of the airplane allowed people to travel more quickly from one place to another and allowed the shipment of perishable goods from one part of the country or world to another.) Then ask students if they think that the technology for space exploration could have been invented without the Wright brothers. (Responses will vary but should get at the notion that the work of the Wright brothers paved the way for the technology that enabled us to explore space.)

Invite students to conduct some research about the technology that was needed to launch space exploration. Students may wish to work in small groups to write a report about this technology and what resulted from its invention.

# AMELIA TAKES TO THE SKIES
**by Navidad O'Neill**
**Pages 103–107**

---

*Use with Chapter 10, Lesson 1*

## Objectives

☐ *Recognize the contributions Amelia Earhart made to the field of aviation.*

☐ *Identify the qualities that this explorer possessed that enabled her to achieve success.*

☐ *Perform a play about Amelia Earhart.*

### Performing a Play

After students have read the play, discuss with them the accomplishments of Amelia Earhart. (She was the first woman to fly solo across the Atlantic; she opened the field of aviation to women.) Then ask students what kind of person they think Amelia was. (brave, curious, extremely competent in terms of understanding how her plane worked and how to repair it) Point out that prior to Amelia Earhart's efforts, the field of aviation was a field dominated by men. Earhart worked very hard to get the field opened to women, so that today in this country there are women pilots and women astronauts.

Have students perform the play. You may wish to divide the class in half so that you can have two casts. Assign parts or ask for volunteers. Students may either memorize their lines or perform the play as Readers Theater. When the performers/readers are satisfied with their efforts, they may wish to present their play to another class.

# THE FIRST RIDE: BLAZING THE TRAIL FOR THE PONY EXPRESS

## by Jacqueline Geis
## Pages 108–112

---

*Use with Chapter 10, Lesson 2*

---

## Objectives

☐ *Identify the role the Pony Express played in communication during the early days of our country.*

☐ *Write a poem about the Pony Express.*

### Writing a Poem

After students have read the selection, ask them to discuss how the Pony Express worked. (It was set up like a relay, with riders riding for a period of time and then passing the mail to the next rider.) Then ask students to speculate about what life must have been like for the riders. (It was a rugged and hard life, requiring a great deal of stamina and perseverance.) *What did the Pony Express require of its riders?* (They had to promise not to use bad language, drink alcohol, or fight with other riders.) *What brought on the end of the Pony Express?* (the arrival of telegraph lines in California)

Have students write a poem about the Pony Express. Students can brainstorm ideas in small groups, using the selection for images and ideas. Then each group can collaborate to write a poem. Encourage students to share their poems with the class.

# MUSIC, MUSIC FOR EVERYONE

## by Vera B. Williams
## Pages 114–119

---

*Use with Chapter 11, Lesson 1*

---

## Objectives

☐ *List ways people can help one another.*

☐ *Identify how people earn money and save for what they need.*

☐ *Draw storyboards for a video of Music, Music for Everyone.*

### Drawing Storyboards with Captions

After students have read the story, have them list ways that the characters help one another. (Rosa takes care of her sick grandmother and plays music for her; music teachers help the band pick pieces to play; Aunt Ida helps the band practice; Leora's mother invites the band to play at the party; the band entertains people at the party; Leora's mother pays the band for playing at the party.)

Then ask students to think about why Rosa wished to earn money. (The family money jar was empty; money was needed to help Rosa's grandmother.) Point out that Rosa offered a service to her community for which she earned money. Encourage students to talk about other services and goods a community offers.

Divide the class into small groups to plan a video of the story *Music, Music for Everyone*. After identifying the various scenes in order, each group should create storyboards for the video by making drawings of each scene, including its characters and setting. The groups should also write captions for each scene on the storyboard, explaining what takes place in the scene. You might hang up the storyboards around the room and invite students to discuss similarities and differences among them.

# ON THE JOB
**Selections from Interviews by Linda Scher**
**Pages 120–121**

*Use with Chapter 11, Lesson 2*

## Objectives

- ☐ *Recognize the contributions of various types of workers.*
- ☐ *Identify characteristics of various jobs.*
- ☐ *Interview a worker about his or her job.*

## Writing an Interview

After students have read the selection, discuss the three jobs that are described. *Which job is most appealing to you?* (Responses will vary, but encourage students to offer reasons for their choices.) *What is the most exciting part about the produce manager's job? The most difficult?* (meeting people; satisfying every customer) *What is the best part of the veterinarian's job? The most challenging?* (working with children; educating people about the needs of their pets) *What is the best part of the anchorperson's job? The most difficult?* (the job is never boring; you don't always know what you're going to do next) Ask students what other jobs they would be interested in learning more about.

Have students interview someone in the community about his or her job. Students can first decide whom they would like to interview and then write three or four questions to ask that person. Encourage students to report their findings to the class.

# UNCLE JED'S BARBERSHOP
**by Margeree King Mitchell**
**Pages 122–125**

*Use with Chapter 11, Lesson 2*

## Objectives

- ☐ *Identify the difficulties faced in opening a business.*
- ☐ *Recognize that small businesses are part of our nation's economy.*
- ☐ *Create a plan for a small business.*

## Creating a Plan

After students have read the selection, discuss with them what Uncle Jed's dream was. (He wished to own his own barbershop.) *Why did it take him a long time to achieve his dream?* (He gave his first savings to his niece so that she could have an operation; he lost his second savings in the Great Depression.) *When did he open his barbershop?* (on his seventy-ninth birthday) Then ask students to think of their community. *What small businesses are part of it? Why do you think these businesses are important?* (Responses will vary, but students should understand that small businesses are an important part of communities, offering goods and services that larger businesses sometimes cannot.)

Have students create a plan for a small business of their own. Students can work in small groups to plan their businesses. Encourage students to think about how much money they would need to start their business and what it would look like. Students may wish to share their plans with the class.

# THE COW
**by Robert Louis Stevenson**
**Page 126** 🔲

Use with Chapter 12, Lesson 1

## Objectives

□ *Recognize how the poet uses language to describe something about farming that has not changed.*

□ *Write a description of a dairy farm.*

## Writing a Description

After students have read the poem and listened to it on the cassette, call upon volunteers to read it aloud. Ask students to discuss the images in the poem. *What do you see? What does the cow look like? What do you think the farm looks like?* (Responses will vary but should mention some of the descriptions in the poem.) Ask students to discuss whether they think this image is typical. (There are some small farms left in the United States, but many farms today are large and automated.)

Have students write a description of a dairy farm. Students can use images from the poem and can also consult reference books to find information about dairy farming today. Encourage students to share their findings with the class.

# PICKING BERRIES
**by Aileen Fisher**
**Page 127** 🔲

Use with Chapter 12, Lesson 1

## Objectives

□ *Appreciate the way that strong rhythms and repeated words in a poem can convey the sense of a repetitive job.*

□ *Recognize that people can sometimes make their work easier by finding the fun in it.*

□ *Write a poem about a familiar task.*

## Writing Your Own Poem

After students have listened to the cassette, have them read the poem aloud. Point out that the poet repeats words such as *picked* and *picking*. Ask students why they think the poet used these repetitions. (to stress the repetitive nature of the work) To make the poem even more realistic, you might have students make a picking motion with their hands each time the words appear in the poem.

Ask students to think of times when they do a repetitive task, such as pulling weeds, sweeping floors, or drying dishes. Ask students: *How do you feel about the work? Is it at all fun? Have you ever invented games or made up a song to make the work seem easier or go faster?* Then have students write a poem about some repetitive task. They might want to find a way to convey the repetitive nature of the work through their choice of words and rhythms.

# DOWN IN A COAL MINE

**Folk Song**
**Page 128** 📼

---

*Use with Chapter 12, Lesson 2*

## Objectives

- ☐ *Recognize that the song conveys both the difficult work of a coal miner and the pride miners take in their work.*
- ☐ *Research the uses of coal today.*
- ☐ *Reach conclusions about the importance of coal and coal miners to our country today.*

### Building Knowledge

Have the class read along as they listen to the song on cassette. Then have them sing along by joining in on the choruses. Afterward, discuss what coal-mining work is like. (dark, back-breaking, long hours, dirty, no good air to breathe) *Why would people who do this kind of work sing such a happy song?* (perhaps to cheer each other up) Point out the last line of the second verse: "What would our country be without the lads that look for coals?" It suggests that one of the things that keeps the miners going is the pride they have in doing something important for our country.

Have students find out more about the uses of coal today. Then have them list on a class poster the information they find. Encourage them to draw conclusions about the role of coal and coal miners in our country.

# WORKING ON AN ASSEMBLY LINE

**by Chuck Hilt**
**Page 129–130**

---

*Use with Chapter 12, Lesson 3*

## Objectives

- ☐ *Identify how the selection makes clear that assembly-line work is like participating in a team sport.*
- ☐ *Plan the questions for an interview with Chuck Hilt.*

### Background

Tell students that in 1913 Henry Ford, searching for the cheapest way to build cars, set up the first successful assembly line in our country. Soon after, assembly lines became an important part of mass production in the United States. Today robots are used to do some of the work that was once done by people on assembly lines.

### Writing an Interview

After students have read the selection, discuss how assembly-line work resembles playing a team sport. You might ask students to try a simple assembly-line activity, such as collating papers into stacks or putting together a batch of sandwiches. Discuss how their experience was like Chuck Hilt's and how it was different.

Ask students to suppose that they could interview Chuck Hilt about his life and work. *What would you ask him?* Have them write down at least five questions to ask him and tell them to be prepared to explain why they would ask each question.

# NO STAR NIGHTS
**by Anna Egan Smucker**
**Pages 131–134**

*Use with Chapter 12, Lesson 3*

## Objectives

☐ *Identify the natural resources used for making steel.*

☐ *Recognize the beauty in the mill town described by Anna Smucker.*

☐ *Design a poster based on some of the descriptions of Weirton in No Star Nights.*

## Creating a Chart

After students have read the selection, discuss the various ways in which Anna Smucker describes her life in a mill town. Discuss with students how the writer sees beauty in her harsh surroundings. Have students skim the story to find the vivid descriptions that Smucker uses to create images of Weirton. (turned the darkness into a red glow; golden spark-spitting steel; great puffy clouds of red, orange, and yellow)

Ask students to create a chart listing how the use of natural resources affected life in Weirton. Suggest that students skim the selection to find ways that the steel mill affected the environment. (For example, *because of smoke from the mill's smokestacks:* everything was a rusty red color, school windows were kept shut; *because of loose graphite:* students had to protect themselves in windy weather; classrooms needed to be dusted every day; and so on.) After students have completed the chart, display it on the bulletin board.

# WHAT A WONDERFUL WORLD
**by George David Weiss and Bob Thiele**
**Page 135**

*Use with Chapter 12, Global Connections*

## Objectives

☐ *Recognize the imagery in the song and what it expresses about nature.*

☐ *Write an alternate verse to the song.*

## Writing a Verse

Have students read the lyrics to the song. Ask them to talk about the different images of nature in the song. (trees of green, red roses, skies of blue, colors of the rainbow) Discuss what these images have in common. (They show nature as being beautiful and wonderful.)

Have students think of other beautiful images in nature. Ask them to write a variation of a verse or a new verse using these images. It may help to have students substitute a few words of the existing line. (For example, the first line could be changed from "I see trees of green, red roses too" to "I see fields of grass, blue flowers too.") Besides friends and family, ask students for whom they might like to sing their new song and why.